BEYOND FEAR AND RAGE

BEYOND FEAR AND RAGE

Ervin Laszlo

CONTENTS

FOREWORD

We must find ways that allow our human intellects to commune with the highest energies in the universe to reach new levels of understanding that will result in effective solutions to current problems. The time for complacency is long past. The time for conventional thinking is also past. The time for compassion combined with radical thought is upon us. Radical thought alone is not going to achieve measurable results. We must include compassion that looks at the entire system of consciousness that has created our universe. It does not matter what political or religious or spiritual belief you hold. It does not matter if you are an atheist. There are universal laws and principles which govern all behavior and all creation. Humans are no exception. For lack of a better word, we might describe the fundamental law of the universe as the law of compassion. The law of compassion dictates that all beings have the right and desire to continue to exist and evolve in their highest form. At times the expression of this law is the transformation of the system of being to its next level of evolution. This is the kind of breakthrough-thinking that is required if we are to overcome the increasingly hysterical behavior that threatens our planet and the many significant accomplishments of human beings over the last two thousand years.

This book is a call to action. It is a compendium of inspirational messages by many of the thought leaders of our time and it offers meaningful direction for the dialogues that must take place if we are to overcome the fear and the rage of many layers of the population, and the blunders of those who have been entrusted with making choices in government, education, health, technology, economics, and social welfare—choices that will determine the future of wellbeing on this planet. We must find new ways to collaborate and communicate, so as to create a just, robust, flourishing system for all of us who are fortunate to be part of the expanding consciousness now manifesting on this planet.

William and Gayle Gladstone

PREFACE

Extraordinary conditions call for extraordinary responses. Fear and rage spreading among wide layers of the population is an extraordinary response, but it is a gut-response and not a good response. Rage leads to deepening confrontation and ultimately to violence, and fear allows confrontation to blossom without doing anything about it. One is active and the other passive, but they have the same end-result: the situation gets worse.

A good response is not a gut-response but an informed response. There are sources of information that do not call for a graduate degree in quantum physics and mathematical economics to access. The insights offered at the cutting edge of science are such information. They are simple and basic, even if the experiments and the reasoning that have led to them are complex. Likewise, the information conveyed by deep and lived spirituality is fundamental, and it is meaningful in itself. Remarkably, and entirely significantly, these two sources of information convey the same, or at least an entirely compatible, insight. We are linked beyond the conventional limits of space and time, and we are one. Comporting ourselves in light of this insight is good for each of us and good for all of us. Acting in light of this insight is the informed response to the extraordinary conditions in which we find ourselves.

The Messages conveyed in this Manifesto are by leading exponents of the new paradigm at the cutting edge of contemporary science and lived spirituality. They are not dogmatic precepts, or even handy recipes for resolving one problem or another. They are explorations and examples of the thinking we need to understand the nature of the problems and their possible solutions—and then having the light and the motivation to find the solution by ourselves. This is the kind of thinking that can replace irrational fear and blind rage with deeper understanding and informed behavior. It can orient

ERVIN LASZLO

our aspirations, our values, and thus our steps. In these extraordinary times it is the kind of thinking we need—in our and in humankind's most urgent self-interest.

Ervin Laszlo

Fighting the darkness ensnares us in an eternal battle.
Transcending the battle is the only way forward.

Deepak Chopra

MESSAGES BY THE AUTHORS OF
*WHAT IS REALITY**

*   *What Is Reality? The New Map of Cosmos and Consciousness.* Ervin Laszlo with
     Alexander Laszlo. New York: Select Books, 2016

JOHN R. AUDETTE

Eternea, Inc.

The future beckons. What will we make of it? At this unique juncture in human history, we have a rare opportunity to achieve something extraordinary. We have the opportunity to make a collective choice to achieve greatness embodying our highest and best visions for a truly remarkable, magnificent future.

Alternatively, we can choose instead to squander hope for a brighter future in timid acquiescence to a highly pathological status quo, which for most thinking human beings has become unacceptable, inexcusable, and intolerable. This moment is now our time of choosing and choose we must, just as nature is beginning to choose for us with so many stark geo-physical warnings and unmistakable shots across our worried bow.

Will we rise to the occasion? One can only hope so, considering that our very survival is at stake. But, if our past is any indication, there is abundant reason to conclude that we might not measure up to the formidable challenges at hand, which urge us now like never before to decidedly evolve or inevitably perish.

Clearly, our record of past deeds is not entirely worthy of praise, admiration or emulation by even basic standards of conduct, decency and civility. To be sure, the cumulative sum of these deeds has today delivered us to the extreme outer edge of the abyss, staring straight into the prospect of our own extinction by our own hand. We could have done better in making our past choices, but we fell short.

What was lacking? What was there to guide us toward better choices then? What could have made a difference in the paths we decided to travel heretofore? No doubt the roads we chose to take in the past have led us to no enviable place. Consider the woeful facts.

We have over-populated and over-polluted our fragile planet, stretching it to the limit of its capacity to sustain us in the manner to which we have become accustomed. We have littered it with nuclear waste and nuclear weapons, any small number of which could bring about our complete and total destruction in an instant. We have exploited the oceans decimating precious coral reefs and many species of marine life. We have killed off many old growth forests too, and many species of plant and animal life along with them. We have created the greatest economic disparity in history, with only a small percentage of humans controlling the lion's share of resources and wealth, relegating with callous disregard no less than half of the human population to squalor, poverty, hunger, disease, oppression, and misery.

Yes, the messy truth of the matter is that we have made some very poor choices historically culminating in our current sub-optimal state of affairs. True, it must be said in fair contrast that we humans also have our redeeming features. Our combined creativity and all that it has spawned: the cumulative contributions of all art forms, architecture, literature, science, technology, music, dance and our courage in the face of dire circumstances, which is where we presently find ourselves, poised on the brink of cataclysmic disasters. For all these reasons, and more, humanity is worth saving and need not be a failed experiment in the universe.

But, sadly, we seem determined to destroy ourselves, much like the poor bloke with advanced lung cancer or COPD who simply refuses to stop smoking. Go figure. The sorrowful evidence continues to mount day after day that we are continuing to make poor choices as a species, macro and micro choices that can only result in a repetition of a grossly dysfunctional past with horrific outcomes that most reasonable human beings would shudder to contemplate, let alone actually experience in reality.

Yet we need not be enslaved by the past, or shaped by it, unless we insanely choose to trade self-inflicted mediocrity for the bliss of an optimal future for earth and all its inhabitants. Thus, it begs the question, perhaps the most important question we could and should be asking ourselves at this most urgent and critical time. How can we make better choices as a species, micro and macro? What will it take to put us solidly on a true compass heading for an ideal future? What will reshape our values, virtues, attitudes and behavior? What would compel us to make more enlightened choices concerning our future? What will engender a virulent pandemic of empathy, compassion, kindness, sensitivity, love, caring, goodness and generosity equally shared by all human beings toward one another, our planet and all things thereupon?

A global strategy is needed to address this challenge. If one is found, and pray it will, it will be found none too soon, for the clock is about ready to strike midnight from all appearances. Eternea.org proposes one such potential strategy, which if nothing else at least deserves serious consideration by all those in search of a viable solution.

Eternea's current chairman, Ervin Laszlo, has chosen this U.S. based non-profit organization to be the primary vehicle through which he and the Eternea team intend to build public awareness of what he calls the "New Paradigm," explained in depth in his last book entitled *What Is Reality?*, an important attempt to further the advancement of human thinking and behavior.

Our deeply troubled world today is predominately secular, mostly forsaking that which is truly sacred. In large part, this is due to flawed thinking and perceptions about the nature of reality, fed over the last three centuries or so by the materialist model of science. As Laszlo's last book and others before it clearly demonstrate, this time-worn model is now empirically invalid and demonstrably archaic. It no longer serves the quest for truth to give credence to it, or the quest to build an optimal sustainable future for earth and all its inhabitants. To continue promoting the false belief that this physical existence and the physical observable universe is all there is and nothing more would be perpetuating the greatest of all crimes against humanity and its hopes to build an ideal future for earth and all its inhabitants.

If we are to have any chance at a future worth living, we must reject the materialist model, and soon, in favor of one based on harmony, unity, love, beauty, kindness, inter-connectedness, and the truth of our eternal existence as spiritual beings, owing not to the overreaches of faith or the stern imposition of rigid dogmas, but rather built solidly on a convergent model of knowledge derived in part from the scientific study of spiritually transformative experiences and non-local consciousness experiences.

The findings from these studies give us compelling and credible basis to develop the abiding conviction that Laszlo's New Paradigm is indeed worthy of our enduring confidence, further reinforced by Eternea's Seven Core Statements and Fifteen Insights. These insightful resources could offer the orientation we need to head in a new hopeful direction.

The future is indeed ours to see. We co-create it every minute of every day by the choices we make. We can no longer afford the chronic curse of making poor choices, one after another. Rather, if we want to have any future worth living, it is now imperative that we make consistently enlightened choices in service to the greater good of all things, informed by the New Paradigm and reinforced by Eternea's Statements and Insights.

CHRISTOPHER M. BACHE

Youngstown State University

Every clear thinking person knows the challenges we are facing: expanding world population, unchecked industrial pollution, climate change, rising sea levels, destabilized weather patterns, collapsing water tables, species extinction, fished out oceans, shrinking nonrenewable resources, unstable interlocked national economies, extreme economic inequality, unprecedented refugee migrations, cities going bankrupt, and no end in sight. Each year we see more clearly that we are driving our planet into a state of such overload that humanity is hovering on the brink of an abyss.

I am a philosopher of consciousness, and I will speak here from my work exploring the deep psyche with psychedelics. When one enters deep states of consciousness in carefully structured psychedelic sessions, insights into the global crisis we are facing sometimes surface and a strange paradox presents itself. While the shadow of the global systems crisis has grown steadily darker for decades now, the vision of the future that has consistently come forward in my sessions, and in the sessions of other people I know, is that humanity is rapidly approaching a breakthrough of evolutionary proportions. Despite the fact that we have repeatedly failed to heed the ecological warnings and reign in our rapacious greed, the message that comes through is one of promise and hope. More than hope, a message of emerging greatness. Solving this paradox requires that we penetrate to the core of this crisis and understand what it represents at the deepest level.

The environmental, social, economic, and political challenges we are confronting are at their core challenges of consciousness. Our culture was built by a species that has reached a specific stage of its psychological development,

7

the stage of the egoic self. The old paradigm enshrines egoic consciousness as normative, but while it empowers great individual accomplishment, it is also profoundly limited. It has not yet penetrated beneath individual consciousness to discover the ground of consciousness where all life is sourced in the Oneness the new paradigm describes. Individuals have tapped into this Oneness, but collectively our species still floats on the surface of the deep psyche, trapped in the narrow confines of self-interest and self-cherishing, cut off from the deeper rhythms of life. A species that is only individually self-aware creates a world that is divided, that works for some but at terrible cost to others. And now we discover that this divided world is deeply unsustainable. Our global culture built by ego is doomed.

My visionary experience over many years has been that the creative intelligence of the universe is attempting to take our entire species to a higher stage of maturational development and that the global systems crisis is an evolutionary driver in this process. What I have seen is that humanity is coming into a Great Awakening—a fundamental shift in our values, understanding, and empathy, a shift in the very foundation of consciousness, in the collective unconscious itself. This will be a true before-and-after moment in history. But for there to be a Great Awakening of this magnitude, there must first take place a Great Death. We will have to surrender the beliefs and practices that divide us and replace them with more inclusive beliefs and practices. We will have to exchange a narrow definition of our self-interest for an enlarged sense of collective purpose.

In spiritual circles, the "dark night of the soul" is a period of intense purification that precedes spiritual realization. In *Dark Night, Early Dawn,* I argued that we have entered the dark night of our collective soul, a time of collective purification and transformation that will last generations. Forecasters tell us that the global systems crisis will be so severe that it will eventually force us to reassess everything in our lives. Events we can no longer control will take from us many of what we consider the normal and necessary structures of our life, forcing us to let go of what can be assumed at deeper and deeper levels. But through this ordeal I believe nature is giving birth not only to a new civilization but to a new order of human being. Through this long crisis, humanity will be changed at its core. Breakdown will trigger breakthrough. Under the press of such widespread disruption, violence will no doubt increase, but in the end I believe compassion will win out because compassion is rooted in Oneness and Oneness is the universal truth rising in history. As our hearts and minds open to Oneness, we will enter into deeper communion with each other and with the living Cosmos itself.

In a time of accelerated change when old certainties are falling away, it is only natural that people would try to hold on to the past, that we would be drawn to leaders who promise to take us back to a more stable time and more familiar order. If we were desperate enough, we might even elect leaders who deny scientific consensus and reassert the old divisions of race and religion. But denial will not hold back the oceans and racial stereotypes that lead to Auschwitz and Dachau.

This century is a race between our past and our future, between the divisions of history and the vision of an integrated planet. I believe that in the end the future will win, but I fear we will suffer terribly before we reach safe harbor. We have deferred taking action on too many fronts for too long to escape the consequences of our delay. But as hard as our circumstances may become, our collective suffering will accelerate this evolutionary transition. In the highly charged conditions of the near future, nonlinear dynamics will replace linear dynamics allowing innovative synergistic change to emerge faster than expected.

If the private ego is dying, what is taking its place? In Laszlo's *What is Reality?* we see that many of its contributors accepted reincarnation as a fact of life, and this is a critical piece. What was not discussed, however, is where reincarnation is currently taking us. My visionary experience has persuaded me that in the relentless gathering and integrating of experience century after century, reincarnation is now bringing us to an evolutionary threshold. In the constant folding and refolding of human experience, something new is being fashioned, not simply by adding layers one by one but eventually by *fusing all these layers into a new form of life.* When this happens a higher order of individual identity will emerge on the planet, and sooner than we might think. Under the enormous pressure of the global systems crisis, I think a species stuck at the level of ego will give birth to its next evolutionary expression—a fully embodied soul consciousness. I call this the birth of the Diamond Soul. This is where I think nature is taking us. This is the awakening that will truly change history and make our planet safe for all life.

ALLAN COMBS

California Institute of Integral Studies

The late great American philosopher Richard Rorty wrote two decades ago:

> Members of labor unions, and unorganized unskilled workers, will sooner or later realize that their government is not even trying to prevent wages from sinking or to prevent jobs from being exported. Around the same time, they will realize that suburban white-collar workers—themselves desperately afraid of being downsized—are not going to let themselves be taxed to provide social benefits for anyone else. At that point, something will crack. The non-suburban electorate will decide that the system has failed and start looking around for a strongman to vote for—someone willing to assure them that, once he is elected, the smug bureaucrats, tricky lawyers, overpaid bond salesmen, and postmodernist professors will no longer be calling the shots … One thing that is very likely to happen is that the gains made in the past forty years by black and brown Americans, and by homosexuals, will be wiped out. Jocular contempt for women will come back into fashion …. All the resentment which badly educated Americans feel about having their manners dictated to them by college graduates will find an outlet.
>
> *Achieving Our Country: Leftist Thought in Twentieth-Century America* (Harvard University Press, 1998, pp. 89–90)

Today the world is filled with reactionary leaders and movements. England's withdrawal from the European Union is just one example, as are many illiberal political movements in Europe, the Middle East, South America, and Asia. It is clear that we are living in a dark time, a time of the *fourth turning*[1] (e.g., Howe & Strauss, 1991), or poetically speaking the *Kali Yuga*, characterized in the Indian epic *The Mahabharata* as a period when the

> World Soul is Black in hue; only one quarter of virtue remains, which slowly dwindles to zero at the end... Men turn to wickedness; disease, lethargy, anger, natural calamities, anguish and fear of scarcity dominate. Penance, sacrifices and religious observances fall into disuse. All creatures degenerate. Change passes over all things, without exception.
>
> [https://grahamhancock.com/dmisrab6/]

The heralding of this time of darkness was recently announced in the U.S. presidential election. This was the most thunderous event in American and perhaps even world affairs since the beginning of WWII. On the one hand it marks the deepest descent into the *Kali Yuga*, and on the other, it offers the dim but conceivable promise of the reorganization of a political and economic world gone wrong in many ways. This more optimistic side is emblemized by the mythic image of the "gray champion." A dramatic figure that steps out of the background to face a corrupt political regime.

In 1837 Nathanial Hawthorne wrote of such a specter:

> One afternoon in April 1689, as the American colonies boiled with rumors that King James II was about to strip them of their liberties, the King's hand-picked governor of New England, Sir Edmund Andros, marched his troops menacingly through Boston. His purpose was to crush any thought of colonial self-rule. To everyone present, the future looked grim. Just at that moment, seemingly from nowhere, there appeared on the streets the figure of an ancient man with the eye, the face, the attitude of command. His manner combining the leader and the saint, the old man planted himself directly in the path of the approaching British soldiers and demanded that they stop. The solemn, yet warlike peal of that voice, fit either to rule a host in the battlefield or be raised to God in prayer, were irresistible.

11

At the old man's word and outstretched arm, the roll of the drum was hushed at once, and the advancing line stood still. Inspired by this single act of defiance, the people of Boston roused their courage and acted. Within the day, Andros was deposed and jailed, the liberty of Boston saved, and the corner turned on the colonial Glorious Revolution."

Twice-Told Tales. Nathaniel Hawthorne (1837, p.11)

Boston: American Stationers.

Real persons as objects of heroic projections often present troubling sides as well. In the case of the recent election much has been said in this vein already and it will not be further belabored here.

We are all heading into turbulent times. What lessons have we learned that we can carry with us? What are the implications for conscientious citizens in today's world? The following list offers the suggestions of futurist and humanitarian Robert Theobald, written down in 1999 shortly before his death in Seattle, Washington:

a) People are Ready. Our priority task is no longer to inform people about the need for change but rather to enable them to express their hopes. There is, fortunately, a rapidly growing awareness of the need to listen and work with those with whom one disagrees.

b) Dream no Small Dreams. We shall only attract large-scale positive energy if we enable people to believe that their actions may make a real difference to their children and grandchildren.

c) See the Whole Picture but Act on a Part of it. Big changes happen when a lot of people do a lot of things a little bit differently.

d) Less is More. The threshold for involvement should be set as low as possible so people can start with small steps.

e) Resilience. This is one word, of many, to express the core skill we need in the future. We must move away from brittle, overstressed systems to opportunities for people and ecologies to have time and space for good choices. This leads to co-intelligence rather than co-stupidity.

f) Care for Others and Ourselves. The transformation now occurring is immensely stressful. We need to use spiritual practices to keep ourselves centered. This challenge is particularly great for those who are committed to being in the "empty center:" connecting people and groups but not controlling their actions. We must, in particular, be aware how our patterns of thought, meetings and actions can exclude others: we must constantly respect the different processes that a respect for diversity requires. [2]

JUDE CURRIVAN

Cosmologist, healer, author

Looking back over the arc of the last forty years or so, there has been significant progress in general well-being across the world. On individual levels, too, the so-called mind-body-spirit movement has enabled ever more people to undertake their own personal development on inner and outer levels.

Yet, for very many such well-being has not materialized and unresolved problems have become even more chronic and acute. Despite numerous warning signs over recent years we have been in a state of shared denial during which we couldn't, didn't or wouldn't recognize the increasingly untenable realities of these issues.

In 2016 though, for our collective psyche the pain has become unbearable and neither the unsustainable *status quo* nor denial of its unsustainability are any longer viable options if we are to survive and thrive as a species. We have come to what doctors call a healing crisis.

The world events playing out through this turbulent time are literally mirroring the agony of our unhealed psyche; yet also and vitally, the hope and possibilities that await its healing. Our behaviors are ultimately driven by what we believe about ourselves, each other and the wider world, and whether true or false. Those behaviors then compel their consequences and further behaviors in continuing spirals of escalation or de-escalation.

Our prevailing and predominantly shared beliefs about the world are a "dis-membered" perception of a fragmented and dualistic Universe. We dance the appearance of our believed dualities in their myriad forms of light and shadow, and along their spectrums of perceived inclusions and separations. The same unresolved emotional traumas and fears that ultimately arise from our perspectives of separateness. and the behaviors that derive from them, play out not only in our own lives, but on larger holographic levels of families and friends, ethnic, social and cultural groups, nations and throughout our collective psyche.

Our traumas and fear-based behaviors are responses to our believed and thereby experienced fragmentations between our personal inner and outer lives, between ourselves and others, and with the wider world. They are the symptoms of our "dis-eased" worldview which have brought us to our current crisis.

Yet, as any doctor knows, trying to deal with the symptoms of a disease without actually addressing the root cause will not, cannot, heal it. As long as we adhere to our fragmented beliefs about the nature of reality, we will continue the interplay of perceived duality in a continuing tug of war between different sides. Their teams may have changed through time and circumstance, yet the tug of polarities goes on and on. Those who see themselves as winners in life continue to deny and perpetuate the unfairness, the inequalities and cruelties of existence. Those more who lose out in such situations, continue to strive and suffer. Now however competing imperatives of population expansion, technological advances, aspirational materialism and environmental degradation made the behavioral symptoms of our collective dis-ease globally unsustainable.

Whilst the consequences of our believed separations are very real in our experiences of inequalities, injustices, conflicts and environmental degradations—what if those beliefs were fundamentally wrong? What if we could re-member the true and essentially unified nature of reality? And if so, what would it mean to us and to how we treat ourselves, each other, and our planetary home?

In today's collective crisis we have a fundamental and unavoidable choice. We either cling to our dis-membered and duality-based worldview, facing the likelihood of a catastrophic breakdown. Or, we can wake up to re-member the ultimate unity of reality and come together in a collective breakthrough.

Complex systems, such as our global society and its underpinning by our collective psyche, when sufficiently destabilized may exhibit what is known as flickering. During such a process the system wobbles or flickers between alternative states before undergoing a sudden transition to one or the other.

The crisis of our time exhibits such flickering; where the despair of the old, unsustainable and breaking system is illuminated by the flickering of hope, emerging throughout the world. The courage, dreams, intentions and actions of a higher more coherent state of shared consciousness become empowered and are increasingly able to manifest themselves. A key contribution to the nascent indications of such hope is emerging at the leading-edge of scientific research.

Hitherto, science's materialistic and reductionist mainstream perspective has directly or indirectly supported and indeed reinforced our dis-membered view of the world. Recent discoveries, however, ranging from cosmology, information theory and complex systems analyses to biology and quantum physics, are accumulating and they are converging in a 21st century scientific revolution.

The latest scientific insights are showing that the digital information whose existence, flows and interactions are the basis of our technologies, is *exactly* the same as the universal in-formation that *is* all that we call physical reality. Moreover, scientific research is progressively demonstrating that from dynamic informational patterns embedded on a holographic boundary and arising from deeper super-physical realms our entire Universe exists and evolves as a unified entity. Our Universe is literally "in-formed" and holographically realized.

The informational science of this emergent whole worldview not only restates, expands and reconciles the understanding of our physical Universe, but unifies reality by its inclusion of supernormal phenomena and universal spiritual experience, revealing that mind *is* matter and consciousness is not something we *have*; it is what we and the whole world *are*. The radical re-envisioning of not only *how* the world is as it is, but *why* the whole worldview grounds physical reality in more fundamental realms of intelligence, causation and meaning, provides a crucial context and vital validation of the flickering of hope.

By empowering us collectively to heal our fragmented perspectives and so to transform the behaviors that arise from them, the whole worldview invites and inspires us to co-create sustainable, just and peaceful solutions to global issues, valuing, empathizing with and celebrating our diversity whilst understanding, experiencing and ultimately embodying the unity that is the true nature of reality.

KINGSLEY L. DENNIS

Laszlo Institute of New Paradigm Research

We have entered times of incredible change, readjustment, and upheaval. There are many contrary forces pushing through our diverse societies and straining to breaking point the incumbent structures and institutions that, in many cases, are no longer functional for progress. Politics—*politikos*, of, for, or relating to, citizens—is in a sense the science of community. It is also an expression of the science of the soul; it reflects the state of human consciousness, and the political sphere provides a vessel for the growth and transformation of the human being. Our social communities are the incubators for the enhancement and expansion of human consciousness.

Political and social theories and practices do not exist in a philosophical and psychological vacuum. Importantly, they are related to two important factors: i) the human being's worldview, and view of the universe, and ii) the human being's view of himself or herself. A concept of society, government and justice always rests on the conceptions we have of the cosmos and our place in it.

The orderly medieval worldview was held together by a largely coherent religious cosmological system. This was then replaced by a scientific paradigm held together by a Cartesian-Newtonian cosmological doctrine. And yet in our modern age of scientific-psychological exploration we are witnessing the demise of this once-dominant consensus. To put it plainly, as a species we are lacking any coherent cosmological view to provide us with meaning and significance. Human consciousness is lacking a coherent and shared vision, which in turn affects how we project ourselves onto society and within socio-political discourse. C.G. Jung said that "Every advance in culture is psychologically an extension of consciousness." Likewise, an extension of human consciousness lacking coherence and meaning projects dissonance into our societies. This is why it is imperative we adopt a new map of reality that can provide us with a new cosmology and worldview that has meaning for our times. Especially as we are on the cusp of transitioning into a diverse yet hopefully unified planetary civilization.

Modern western society places little or no value upon the inner experience, thus placing no value or focusing attention upon the need for conscious evolution, preferring to dwell within a largely economic rationalization of the world. In this worldview the human ego exalts the individual personality at the expense of compassionate relations, empathy, and connectedness. It is the ego which propels a minority of voices on the world stage to declare separatism, division, and national self-interests over and above the need for international cooperation, collaboration, compassion, and understanding. It is this rhetoric which gives the opportunity for a hitherto neglected section of society to come forward through the expression of repressed anger and the unleashing of chaotic, disruptive energy. It also allows for the mindset that economic and political changes and upheavals are able to solve all problems because the source of such ills is in the objective environment rather than in the consciousness of the human being. And yet whilst the projection of peoples' anger and negativity onto others creates the illusion of improvement, it is actually an unhealthy mechanism that fails to address the real concern. The projection of repressed anger attaches itself to external socio-political movements and charges them with great power—this has long been the bane of human history!

That is why today we are desperately in need of a new understanding—a new map of reality—that allows us to recognize the greater truth. A truth that shows how our material reality is interconnected at the most fundamental level. It is a truth which shows how all living beings are inherently immersed within a collective field of consciousness that resonates between us. We are not separate individuals—isolated islands—but individualized expressions of a unified consciousness that embraces us all at the very core of our being. The new map of the cosmos tells us that the evolutionary trend is toward ever-greater coherence and cohesion, and not it's opposite. It is these aspects which are conducive to a thriving, sustainable future – not the elements of division, conflict, competition, or fear.

If we are to transition into an integrative, coherent phase of human civilization we need to adopt as soon as possible the new paradigm—the new map—that comes at a time when it is most needed. Each person determines his or her conduct within the larger context of the nature of the world and the meaning of human life. We find this context through our ideas—our maps of reality. We need to share the new cosmological understanding through our institutions, our educational systems, and most importantly of all—in our human relations with one another. We are a human family, diverse and yet unified; each an expression of a cosmic oneness that seeks expression within a material reality. We are now called upon to reflect that unity, and to represent the true legacy that is the human race. Our time is now.

SHAMIK DESAI

Laszlo Institute of New Paradigm Research

We live in troubling times. Recent political events around the world confirm that the present age is one of deep anxiety—an anxiety about our identities. There is serious and increased skepticism about cosmopolitanism, globalism, utopianism—ideals which seem to many to provide no visible anchor.

This discomfort with not being sufficiently anchored and rooted in identity has led to a surge in zealous nationalistic feeling across every continent. Geographical boundaries seemingly encase convenient and coherent identities, providing an ostensible comfort zone of selfhood.

However, the present world is misguided in its divisive, fear-mongering approach. Real identity is not shrouded in or confined to a limited space defined by artificial borders. The spirit—the root of our true identities—transcends borders. The "New Paradigm" in science reveals that consciousness is nonlocal and all-pervading, confirming what the ancient wisdom traditions have espoused through millennia—that we are all emanations of a single unified consciousness, and are thus fundamentally One. Our dualistic, "us vs. them" times seem strangely out of sync with what the latest science reveals about the nature of reality.

Embracing our Oneness demands an attitude of universal harmony, compassion, and love. Only when we engage in conscious intention—in loving action—and identify with the creativity that is the inevitable offspring of such action, is our true self revealed. And through such high creative purpose—through "spiritual procreation"—we bend the arc of history toward progress, we hallow the world and collectively elevate the vibrations of the cosmos. Above all, we become more ourselves—deepening and expanding our identities.

The New Paradigm is needed more than ever before. Its purveyors must dare to offer a superior vision to the age-old problem of identity: a global community of called ones—each of us performing our ultimate duty, answering a unique call to heroic and purposeful action in service to humanity.

But to accomplish this successfully in our troubled and turbulent times, the New Paradigm shall have to "show teeth." History has repeatedly taught that as we ascend the ladder of consciousness, we must retain, not lose, the more basic and practical virtues of the preceding rungs. Or we shall tumble down. Evolution, to be sustainable, must "transcend and include."

The New Paradigm must boldly assert itself beyond the confines of a soft, elitist bubble—it must grab the microphone, make itself heard in all quarters, and connect with the "real" people by embedding itself within their sociocultural mores and serving their practical interests. To be effective, the new science in consciousness must enter into the consciousness of the common man. It must speak to him in his own language. The elections across the globe serve as a stark reminder that no degree of cultural sophistication or social finesse, no intellectual accouterment, can compensate for the raw brute strength that must always form the base of the more evolved virtues.

We stand today at a critical crossroads—the choice to pass a great cosmic test and save human civilization is ours. With humanity on the brink of doom—economically, socially, culturally, politically, ecologically—we cannot afford to impoverish it further. We are occupying the "dark night before the new dawn"—the time of Armageddon, of Kali Yuga. The strident and strangled cries pouring from the world's political stage are the sounds of the death knell of an insecure Old Paradigm.

The temporary lowering of the intensity of cosmic vibrations often serves as a catalyst, it demands an enlightened collective response which propels us to the next, higher stage of cosmic evolution. Degeneration brings regeneration. As we synthesize the positive qualities of the dark forces—power, organization, emotionally resonant heroic narrative—we render the other side irrelevant and hence neutralize it, re-integrating civilization at a point of greater coherence. By offering all men and women a glittering 21st century alternative to identity formation—a nobler and fuller vision of themselves—we goad them to heroic creativity rather than "heroic" destruction in the name of a mindless tribalism.

The pendulum of history tends to sweep too far in either direction—our job is to chart the sane, wise course and remain at the vanguard of conscious evolution.

EDE FRECSKA

The University of Debrecen

2500 years ago a poem was born in ancient Greece written in hexameters with the standard metrical line of that era. It described an otherworldly journey of a wise man, "a man who knows," a common title for an initiated mystic. The name of this spiritual traveller was Parmenides of Elea, and the yield of that trip was nothing else but the basic concept of Western philosophy, the very foundation of scientific thinking: the necessity of logical argumentation. It is a paradox of Western thought that its founder was a "iatromantis," a miracle-healer, a priest of Apollo and that it is rooted in a mystical or dream-like state of consciousness. Definitely, as the poem attests, the argument for argumentation has not come developed along the lines of rational thinking. On the contrary: it arose from the obscure depth of a visionary experience, an approach that Western science considers irrational. A spiritual tradition lies at the very roots of Western civilization.

For a long time Parmenides has been recognized among philosophers and historians as the founder of rationalism, the "Father of Logic." While his importance is having laid the foundations of Western science, he has also set path for the whole process of learning and education. However, what he really has done is still more complex and controversial. Parmenides was not just a logician, and most of his teachings were far from rational. He not only outlined the origins of Western culture, but provided a juxtaposition, another approach—an irrational one—he called "the way of truth." This approach is based on direct apperception and takes closer to reality than does reasoning. The latter, which unfolds reality with the help of logos, "the way of opinion," he described as illusory. From what he was teaching about the foundations of knowledge, the West has taken and followed only one. Nevertheless this is what formed the West, and what differentiates it profoundly from the rest of the world, in stark contrast with the traditions of the Far East and thinking in Pre-Columbian America.

Another ancient Greek thinker and "iatromantis," Empedocles of Acragas, was born just a few years after Parmenides, and he also recorded his teachings in the form of poetry. He played a fundamental role in the development of Western culture; Aristotle called him the "Father of Rhetoric." The richness of his style, and the clearness of his descriptions surpasses the expressions of his contemporaries. Like Parmenides, Empedocles was a miracle-healer, using his ability to access altered states of consciousness. Nevertheless, Parmenides and Empedocles were not the only visionary thinkers who made major contributions to Western culture. Pythagoras of Samos, the "Father of Mathematics," has also been considered an "iatromantis," deeply involved in mystical techniques and teachings. Aristotle described Pythagoras as a wonder-worker and something of a supernatural figure. Indeed, it is conceivable that all these Greek philosophers were 'shamans', to use the contemporary anthropological term, drawing their knowledge from trivial cultural traditions. The three founding fathers (of mathematics, of logic, and of rhetoric) Pythagoras, Parmenides, and Empedocles were definitely practitioners and teachers of the shamanic lore, masters of altered, visionary states of consciousness. And yet, strangely enough, they laid the basic foundations of the world and the culture in which we now live.

We cannot stop here: even the founder of modern rational philosophy was not free of visionary influences. On the contrary, Cartesian philosophy is based on three dreams as René Descartes himself admitted. Upon awakening, feeling very troubled by these dreams, Descartes thought that they had been sent to him by Heaven and he searched to find what they meant.

The other mastermind of the Newtonian-Cartesian worldview was himself an ardent practitioner of the mystical lore. Isaac Newton has spent more time on occult and theological studies than on the completion of *Principia Mathematica*: he wrote more than one million words on the subject of alchemy and biblical prophecies and circulated them among likeminded people.

There is no need to emphasize how important these giants were in instigating the scientific revolution that was so influential in shaping the modern world. Yet it is utterly paradoxical that the Founding Fathers of the Age of

Reason have been dealing with pseudoscience and were influenced by irrationality. Also Giordano Bruno, the other forerunner of the contemporary worldview, was more of a mystic than of a scientist.

Although—as these examples illustrate—visionary experiences were profoundly important in shaping our culture, in the course of time their significance has been forgotten. The truth about the real nature of their thought has been distorted and neglected. The paradox does not lie with the thinking of the masters, since they were consistent in following both paths of knowledge: the rational and the so-called irrational. Perhaps the term "irrational" is a misnomer. Two paths of knowledge complement each other in the wisdom teachings. Let us cite here Rabbi Joel David Bakst:

> According to the teachings of esoteric Judaism, all knowledge, both spiritual and material wisdom, originally coexisted in a seamless unity ... Together, these two modes of wisdom comprised a larger, all-encompassing Universal Torah (Torah literally meaning 'instruction' or 'teachings'). A collapse, i.e., the episode of the eating from the Tree of Knowledge, however, ensued in which the database of all knowledge split itself into 'spiritual' and 'material' planes of existence. Thus, we have the roots of the conflict between 'religion' and 'science.' Yet, any given mystical or technological truth can only be one of two sides of the same puzzle. ... The ultimate truth is not revealed through the supranatural alone nor is it only discovered through scientific development—it is more than both.

Nothing is esoteric or strange about these affirmations, they are entirely consistent as part of our cultural origin and to the teachings of the "Founding Fathers" of Western philosophy and science. A certain type of duality and complementarity dynamizes every culture and serves as their foundation: visions and intuitive insights create new knowledge, new values, while logic and language elaborate them. All are equally important and all need special training and techniques to nurture, and they are not interchangeable. The domination of one over the other would stalemate progress in culture.

Despite all of its spectacular achievements, Western culture is worrisomely biased: not only has it lost contact with its source, but it is actually hostile to it. In spite of its material success and apparent sophistication, the West is starving for a real sense of meaning and is unable to to steer its evolution toward a higher spiritual goal. The development is slipping out of our hands. As Peter Kingsley put it: "Unless we touch our roots and make contact again with the essence of our past, we can have no future."

Bakst, J.D. (2016). The messianic role of science and technology.
at http://www.cityofluz.com/messianic-role-science-technology 12/10/2016.
Janaway, C. *Ancient Greek Philosophy I: The presocratics and Plato. In Philosophy: A Guide Through the Subject,* Ed. Grayling, A.C., 336–397. Oxford: Oxford University Press, 1995.
Kingsley, P. In the Dark Places of Wisdom. Inverness: The Golden Sufi Center Press, 1999.
Kingsley, P. Reality. Inverness: The Golden Sufi Center Press, 2003.
Waterfield, R. The First Philosophers: The Presocratics and Sophists. Oxford: Oxford University Press, 2000.

NASSIM HARAMEIN

The Resonance Academy

We live at a critical time in history. We live at a time when humanity's activity within the biosphere has reached a state of imbalance that is quickly tipping towards a cataclysmic outcome. Our social systems and our technological evolutionary path, based on competition and domination, require a fundamental transformation of our understanding of the physics of creation and energy, and the transcendence of our consciousness towards unification.

The path we have been following, although unsustainable in the long term, has been critical for our development, both social and technological, and has led us to the brink of a breakthrough at all levels of our evolution. Driven by social and environmental stresses requiring transformation, we have reached a new understanding of the source of the world and of energy, as well as a deeper understanding of the information network that produces the information feedback loop we experience as self-awareness or consciousness.

These discoveries as well as laboratory studies are telling us something profound about ourselves, the real world around us, and our relationship to it. We live in a highly networked, interconnected, energetic and unified structure that is information driven through electromagnetic fluctuations at the Planck scale. This unifying field of information can no longer be thought of as some esoteric ideology, but is now demonstrated to be the source of mass and of the material world,[1] of energy,[2] and of the information network that drives biological evolutionary processes toward sentient self-aware entities—the entities we interpret as conscious.[3]

Like all significant discoveries in physics, these shifts in our understanding of the world and the source of the world's fundamental forces are ushering in technological advancements that have the potential to completely transform our quest for energy production and transportation and open the door to long-range space travel, and a complete shift in our concept of resources—the shift from scarcity to abundance. Such shifts in our paradigm will reduce, if not alleviate completely, the stressors driven by our belief in the scarcity of resources and energy, which currently lead to territorial and global domination disputes. Yet, in order for this shift to occur, a significant general awareness of unification must be given, allowing our governmental, financial and military-industrial complex to transition in step with the global awareness that is currently emerging. It is, therefore, our greatest responsibility, challenge and opportunity to continue to transform our knowledge base and ourselves to better and deeper encompass both the understanding, and the experience, of a unified, connected universe.

1. Haramein N. Quantum Gravity and the Holographic Mass, *Physical Review & Research International*, ISSN: 2231–1815, pages 270–292, 2012.
2. Haramein N., & Val Baker A. K. F. The Electron and the Holographic Mass Solution, ATINER 4th International Conference of Physics: Abstract Book, page 14, 2016.
3. Haramein N., Brown W., & Val Baker A. K. F. The Unified Spacememory Network: from cosmogenesis to consciousness, *Journal of Neuroquantolog,* 2016.

JEAN HOUSTON

The Jean Houston Foundation

You are, each of you, all in all, a moving hologram of the whole of creation. From what Cosmic Garden of Eden did you emerge? And toward what destiny are you pointed? Perhaps now, as the ground of the known shifts beneath our feet, what we need to steady ourselves is nothing short of a new origin myth, an evolutionary tale that takes visionary science as its given, and places in perspective the "suchness" of our deepest personal reality.

A Meditation on the Metaverse. *In the beginning there were and continue to be the Great Gardeners who live in the Metaverse, a vast farm fertile with energy, creativity, intelligence, and love. The Gardeners decide to plant a new garden in a field of the farm's limitless, nested universes. They begin with an infinitesimally tiny seed, a microcosm coded with the energy resources to flower into a richly varied cosmos. So potent is the ground, so ready is the seed, that once planted, it bursts its pod with an explosion of light and energy.*

And lo, the infinitesimal seed sprouts into a great tree that holds in its branches a trillion galaxies, each blossoming with a hundred billion or more stars. Whirlwinds of energy swirling through the branches coalesce into biosystems of planetary scale, each home to billions of organisms that balance each other in self-sustaining ecological webs. Nourishing each bud of this immense flowering is the great tree, which links every expression of the garden's unfolding in energetic resonance, such that anything that happens in any part is known instantaneously to the whole.

As the budding life forms of the biospheres complexify, the most advanced among them jump first into awareness of themselves and then into awareness of the Great Gardeners who planted them. Problems that arise at each stage of their growth create opportunities for learning, experimentation, and new expression leading the advancing ones to deeper and more profound understanding of themselves and their world. As this understanding grows, they develop ways to meet their physical needs with less and less expenditure of energy and resources, so that more and more of their awareness can be devoted to tending the garden of their consciousness and culture. Soon, the winds of the technology they have evolved are cross-pollinating the flowers of many places and knowings.

Venturing out to explore the worlds of the very large and the very small, first in their imaginations and then through their technological advances, these adventurous ones come to discover the wonders of the cosmic tree. They begin to understand that all life is engaged in a process of continuous creation and that birth, growth, death, and new birth are all expressions of energy in motion. They come to see that the cosmos both within and without is a living organism, a single unified garden, recreated in its entirety moment by moment by the love and intelligence of the Gardeners which flows continuously through the Great Tree like nourishing sap.

They discover, further, that along with the knowledge of the Great Tree comes a radical freedom. They know themselves to be free to make mistakes, to face evil, and to experience suffering, for suffering is the inevitable consequence of the great potential of their seeded nature, locked into a still maturing consciousness. Yet, over time, as their scope of vision widens, these beings evolve toward transcending their suffering. As they do, they come to a more and more expansive understanding of who they are and what they yet may be and do. And this brings the story up to who and what you are in this radical moment of cosmic -earth history dear friends!

Knowing at last that all is within all, the totality present in each part and each part fully connected to the whole, you move beyond the limited conceptions of the local laws of form and gain access to the very patterns of creation. With this knowledge, you, my dear friend, join the Gardeners in their task of planning and planting cosmic gardens and nourishing them with their own intelligence and love. And so, the cosmos continues to bloom.

The cosmic story which I have told here is itself a hologram for living in this critical time. It reminds us that we, too, are Gardeners who can farm the fields of space/time, the generative ground of our being, creating gardens of consciousness, landscapes filled with the blossoms of our minds and spirits. Tending the gardens of your life involves a kind of cosmic yoga; you take yourself back to remembering that you are made of the same stuff as the Metaverse from which you continuously arise, second by second. You share its body, albeit as a manifestation of the Divine Spirit in the world; you are woven into the fabric of its infinite ecology; the productions of your hands and mind—even in the crucible of crisis and finance, are an aspect of its creation and live in eternity. You know yourself, then, as resonant waves of the original seed, an infinite being who contains in your body-mind the design of creation itself, planted in the field of this particular space-time and sustained by a dynamic flow-through of cosmic energy and the love and nurturance of the Divine Spirit.

At your core you already know this to be so. From your reflections and meditations you understand yourself to be a reality surfer, delightedly riding the waves of creation, mind opened, heart expanded, the Metaverse coursing through you. In such states, you are embraced in co-conscious awareness, no longer knowing or caring where "I" leave off and the rest of reality begins, or whether there is any difference. This experience is one of the supreme givens of our nature because the Metaverse in its operational mode is coded into every one of us, but especially in you. The raptures of the deep self are our native equipment, granted you by your cosmic origins. The only requirement is joy and a willingness to say "yes" to the new epic that dawns, right now, in you and me and those fortunate to be alive in the great today. We are seeds coded with cosmic dreams. Bursting the pods of our containment, we are ready to enter into creative partnership with the Metaverse and to populate our particular corner of space-time with our unique vision and capacity.

ALEXANDER LASZLO

The Buenos Aires Institute of Technology (ITBA)

There is hope. Indeed, what is being considered in this manifesto is the collective catalyzing power of the community (the come-union in common-unity) of those whom we might consider the Sourcerers (sic.) of our time—those who tap into, connect with, and are informed by the source. This source is none other than the ground-state background patterning of the cosmos that gives rise to the manifest universe. It is what in some traditions is known as the Akasha.

There is a modern day myth that holds that the Hopi foresaw the rising of such a generation of Sourcerers who they supposedly dubbed the Rainbow Warriors.[1] It is said that these will be peoples, from all walks of life, called upon to usher in the transition of humanity to what in the Hopi cosmology is known as the 5th World.[2]

Without doubt, we are in a time of transition and emergence. A time when the old patterns are being sloughed off, the old structures crumbling, and the old ways of being collapsing. It is a time of new patterns. But before they can arrive, the old patterns must be shaken loose. It is through this shaking that we break free from our chrysalis, that we shed our skin, that we break our eggshell and emerge transformed. This is a painful and chaotic time for our species, but it is also beautiful and awesome. It is the time of the Kali Yuga[3]: "At this time evil comes to the surface to be destroyed."[4] But the destruction of evil is not to be done in the old ways—fighting hatred with hatred, violence with violence, darkness with death. The Sourcerers are called upon to be the change they wish to see in the world—now finally, to embody and enact the values of love, harmony, compassion and Ubuntu.[5] This won't be easy. Indeed, it is nothing short of a cosmic test. Transition to the 5th World envisioned by the Hopi is a birthright of humanity waiting to be claimed. It won't happen as matter of course even though it would be a natural part of the evolution of consciousness on this planet.

According to Anneloes Smitsman, "In moments of deep rest, sleep, and meditation, you can re-enter the unified field of the fifth world behind the four quadrants. Yet many do not remember this, because for many there is not yet a conscious reference for holding this in place. For many, the bridge between the conscious and unconscious domains of your minds have not yet fully formed. The re-unification and re-membering with the unified field of Consciousness takes place when you rest and surrender... You have everything inside you to awaken and find your way Home. It just needs to be brought back into connection, synchronization and harmonization with the unified field from where you have come."[6]

This is a time of re-membering our dance in the web of life—of bringing our membership back into the Council of All Beings,[7] and of re-storying our relationship with the cosmos, weaving a new story built of ancient wisdom and insights born of a connected consciousness. Indeed, this is a Triple Birthing process where we are being called upon to be simultaneously mid-wives of the new constellation, mothers birthing the new constellation, and the new constellation being born—all at the same time! This is the triple role we are being called upon to play into the 5th World.

Evidently, it is less an issue of seeking to heal and humanize the fear-mongering and government-blundering of our times than it is to evolve ourselves and transcend them. Evolutionary pathways involve sloughing off anachronisms, allowing for the dinosaurs to exit gracefully stage left as we nurture the furry evolutionary experiments that emerge in their shadows. As such, this time is far more about breakthrough than it is about breakdown. Of course, both are happening and each of us has a choice as to where to put our energy, our attention, and ultimately our love. This is why the time is one of mid-wifing, of birthing, and of being born—all simultaneously. The essential energies (what are sometimes called the "the core gestures"[8]) of this time are those of an emergent sisterhood among all human beings with all of life's expressions of love and nurturance.

Consciously participating in and curating the conditions for such systems to thrive is a matter of syntony, which in terms of evolutionary systems thinking denotes evolutionary consonance or the occurrence and persistence of an evolutionarily tuned dynamic regime. Through conscious intention aligned with evolutionary purpose, it is possible to embody and manifest conscious evolution. However, this requires a purposeful creative aligning and tuning with the evolutionary flows of our milieu.

The key lies in recognizing and resonating with the harmonics of coherence. Everything vibrates—thoughts, emotions, sensations just as much as the physical world of sight, touch, taste, smell and sound. Sensing the harmonic resonance of each vibrational state—both in and around us—allows us to co-create the coherence domains that support life. Doing so involves tuning into the dynamic regime of the matrix that undergirds life and nurtures the life-enhancing play of emergence. It is a matter of sensing when one expression of reality aligns, harmonizes, resonates and vibrationally syncs with another. Sensing the harmonic overtones and the deep, deep vibrational undertones that reverberate at different pitches within ourselves can bring us into resonant alignment at scalar values of being, from the subatomic to the cosmic. Developing this ability to syntonize, to tune into and consciously align the multiple dimensions of existence, responds to a call to be the change and resolve the dissonance of our times, transcending and transmuting discord into harmony. This requires empathy, intuition, evolutionary consciousness, and above all, agape: the form of universal, unconditional love that transcends and embraces all of creation across time and space. We can do this—indeed, the viability of our species may well depend on our ability to develop and hone our individual and collective sense of syntony.

1. see Willoya, William, and Vinson Brown. Warriors of the Rainbow: Strange and Prophetic Indian Dreams. Healdsburg, California: Naturegraph, 1962; and Niman, Michael I. People of the Rainbow: A Nomadic Utopia. Nashville: University of Tennessee Press, 1997.

2. see Waters, Frank, and Oswald White Bear Fredericks. Book of the Hopi. New York: Ballantine Books, 1963.

3. see Lings, Martin. The Eleventh Hour: The Spiritual Crisis of the Modern World in the Light of Tradition and Prophecy, Cambridge, UK: Archetype, 2002.

4. according to the Great Council of the Grandmothers as reported by Louise Edington on 12 November 2016 http://www.godlikeproductions.com/forum1/message3374057/pg1

5. Mogobe B. The philosophy of ubuntu and ubuntu as a philosophy. In P. H. Coetzee & A. P. J. Roux (Eds.), The African philosophy reader (2nd ed., pp. 230–238). New York/ London: Routledge, 2003.

6. Smitsman, Anneloes. EARTHwise - Love Letters from our Planet. Chapter 7: Our New Future, 2016.

7. Macy, Joanna, John Seed, Arne Naess, and Pat Fleming Thinking Like a Mountain: Towards A Council of All Beings. New Catalyst Books, 2007.

8. see Müller, Cornelia (ed.). Body - Language - Communication, Volume 1, De Gruyter Mouton, Pubs: Frankfurt, Germany, 2013.

ERVIN LASZLO

Laszlo Institute of New Paradigm Research

What can we believe? We have a great deal of information on our fingertips and that is good: the world runs on information. Information in nature is reliable and precise: it is in the form of "laws": the laws of nature. These are instructions, algorithms, that define and determine how things behave in space and in time. They are so precise that a coherent and intelligible universe could emerge from the initial chaos that followed the Big Bang. A difference of just a billionth of the value of some of the "universal constants" of nature—such as the rate of expansion of the universe, the weight of the proton, or the relation of the force of gravitation to the electromagnetic force—would have issued in a sterile universe, where life is physically impossible. But in the human world, information is not so precise and reliable. It is produced by human beings who may be sending or reporting false information, whether by simple error, or as intended misinformation. The human world is filled to the hilt with uncertain, unchecked, and highly questionable information.

Beyond the laws of nature, what information can we believe? The news media whose task it is to convey information of relevance to people's lives is a human institution, manned by communicators who may be conveying faulty information simply because it is what happened to come to their atten-tion—and they did not take the time and make the effort to double and triple-check its source. Presidents and other politicians may also be conveying misinformation on purpose, serving the narrow self-interests of lobbies and of states and of ethnic groups. It is no longer clear whether the political process that determines the social and economic wellbeing of entire nations is based on true information or on intended misinformation. The social media is a precious independent source, but it carries information from a large variety of sources more or less indiscriminately, and while many of these sources are well-intentioned, others could have hidden agendas. How do we know what information we can trust?

The answer is that, in principle, we can trust information based on controlled observation and rigorous reasoning. That is the ideal of what is known as "scientific information." The problem with scientific information, however, is that it is not necessarily relevant to the immediate concerns of people and societies. The information that fills the pages of the thousands of accredited and credible scientific publications needs to be sifted for relevance. In many instances it would have to be actively "relevated"—to use the term introduced by physicist David Bohm. That means placing it into a particular context— *interpreting* it. This is not needed if the information concerns the evolution of the atmosphere of a planet circling Gamma Centauri, for example. But if it touches on human nature, or the nature of nature, it is relevant and requires correct interpretation. How do we know that an interpretation is correct? Most and arguably all, scientific theories allow a variety of interpretations.

There are, of course, laws of scientific reasoning—not everything that we can deduce from observation and experiment is assuredly correct. For one thing, deductions must follow the laws of logic. For another, there is the so-called principle of economy. Known as "Occam's Razor" it tells us that "entities are not to be multiplied beyond necessity"—we must not invoke principles and entities that are not clearly indicated by the evidence. Einstein expressed it well in saying that scientists "seek the simplest possible scheme that can tie together the observed facts." That scheme must be simple and adequate. It must tie together all the observed facts without unfounded assumptions and hypotheses.

But when faced with competing interpretations, with differing and perhaps incompatible and even contradictory claims, the laws of logic alone do not decide the question of correctness. Here, however, we have another criterion we can invoke: the *intrinsic meaningfulness* of the interpretation. This is a cognitive, psychological and hence ineffable factor, beyond the rigorous methods of science, and it was mostly dismissed as irrelevant. Yet it is not necessarily that. The litmus test in regard to intrinsic meaningfulness is the degree to which the information corresponds to our own insights, whether we have formulated them consciously or not. If the interpretation calls forth an "Aha experience"—the sense that yes, this must be the case, I have always known or at least suspected it—then it is more likely to be true than if it is strange and contrary to our intuitions.

The insights accumulated over untold generations in the cultural history of humankind tell us something about the true nature of the things we encounter in our experience. The insights that survive the test of time merit being taken seriously.

The conclusion flowing from these brief but fundamental considerations is that information based on controlled observation and rigorous reasoning, supported by our own insights and intuitions is the information we have the best reason to believe. That is why the insights that bring together the new paradigm in science with sustained spiritual beliefs are likely to be the most reliable kind of information that is available to us. It is our hope, and it has certainly been our sincere intention, that the Messages in this volume convey information of this kind.

The final test, of course, is in the hands of the reader. Is the information carried by these messages veritably based on cutting-edge science, and does it genuinely call forth the "Aha experience" of *"re-cognized"* truth? These queries merit consideration. Perhaps, beyond the welter of untested and purposively or inadvertently dubious information there is a kernel of information about ourselves, our times, and our world that we can truly believe. That would be a ray of light to guide our steps in these chaotic times.

NA AAK

Transpersonal

Reality is simply a mirror image of what lies within our consciousness; all I experience in life corresponds to where my attention rests. My thoughts create reality, my words weave reality, my actions make the tapestry of creation. But can you tell me where is your attention? What are you focused on? This is the matter that concerns us as the waters of the socio-political womb have broken and we have entered into labor.

Our attention is where our consciousness rests and humanity's attention is locked in self-indulgence and self-satisfaction, focused on providing relentlessly all sorts of superficial needs created by religious, social and cultural conceptualizations. This is not because humans are intrinsically bad or faulty, rather our nature is a perfect mathematical flow of information from the Akasha—as mystics say, we are made of light. What creates a distortion of that inner perfection is "ignorance," this condition of our consciousness acts as a veil upon our perception of reality, blinding our senses to the true nature of life. An incarnation in a bardo of ignorance, such as planet Earth, is purposively a step in the ladder of evolution. It brings consciousness into a spiral of awakening until it reaches again a state of enlightened individuation.

What matters is not the destination, but the journey to the destination, the path every consciousness walks towards its liberation from ignorance. This journey called life, is the wonder and pleasure of having all experiences as if they were real, even though they are temporal and relative. The key to the puzzle of this ignorant experience of life is free will, choice, because it means that we are not chained to or locked into any circumstance. The real imprisonment we experience is affliction. When our perception is blind-folded with ignorance, we become hosts to afflictive states of consciousness, fear seeps under the skin making us experience guilt, shame and doubt. Once we allow these parasites to make themselves at home in our body we are no longer ignorant—we become ill.

Not to see is simply a matter of not allowing evolution towards seeing. Ignorance is the vehicle that stops evolution, but affliction is the illness we have to deal with. Affliction becomes the motivator of our thoughts, emotions, words and actions, and when that occurs there is no other possible result but affliction all over again. We all seek change but very few of us are pointing to the core of what needs to be changed. Choosing a different person as president, creating new institutions that regulate the ones that exist, making plans to eradicate hunger, promoting peace are all viable solutions, but they must not be motivated by the affliction. To understand this is of the utmost importance, because ideas are not enough to bring about change, words are not enough to manifest change; what is needed is action, people choosing to be different and to be of service to the collective. These actions are pointless if they are fueled by fear.

Our attention and our motivation is continuously weaving, knitting the intricate tapestry we are experiencing of life. We tend to fall into the drama of being shocked about what takes place in the world. We react as if suddenly bizarre trees would appear in the middle of the road. We walk arrogantly complaining about them, when we were those who prepared the ground, chose the seeds, planted and nourished them with plenty of affliction until they grew into big, tall, and awkward trees in the middle of the road. Cutting the trees down is not a solution—it is simply an action that eliminates the uncomfortable need of having to take responsibility of what is and will always be our own doing. The illness of affliction makes us become enemies of our own kind, despise, dislike and kill all what does not enter into our desired frame of reality, created by a distorted perception of reality. The rest is history, centuries of afflictive beliefs, political states, economic decisions, wars, genocides and what I consider most harmful, an education system that promotes the constriction as opposed to its expansion of the mind.

Time has shifted, the equivalent to one year decades ago probably corresponds to a few hours today. This is a danger if we persist in maintaining our afflictions as the motivator, since we are not walking but rushing into self-extermination. On the other hand this is also where the eye of the needle of our evolution resides, if we choose virtue as the motivator of life and bring our attention to bear on the present moment. Then we could inflict enough pressure on this side of the balance to find the tipping point towards the breakthrough rather than the breakdown of society.

The entire fabric of reality is a huge mantelpiece weaved carefully and intricately, there is no experience that would run separately from the whole of the cosmos. We might fail to see the dots that join one event with another, but this lack of vision does not change the fundamental nature of the continuum of life. Each time my mind has a thought, it creates a thread knitted to another, creates patterns, forms, experiences.

In our lack of consciousness and ignorance we become victims of what is around us, blaming and relentlessly trying to find scapegoats that pay for what we dislike. This is exactly what we are doing now as we observe the current political and social events that have not just attracted our attention, but hijacked our very existence for months. Fear, anxiety, assumptions, presuppositions, forecasts capture our mind. This attitude not only does not help us find solutions but it is weaving the tapestry of our future experience.

We are pronouncing our own death sentence with no possibility to appeal it. If we want change, we must stop knitting affliction! Discernment is the capacity to comprehend what is not visible at first sight but is implicit in the consequences of what we are experiencing. The current political situation is a tree that has grown over time from a seed we all had collectively chosen, planted and nourished. If humanity fails to understand this, no possible and plausible change can take place in reality. To exercise discernment, I need to awaken to the fact that I am ignorant, ill with affliction. My attention has been hijacked by this affliction. Change requires that we exercise discernment, that we live motivated by an unconditional regard for life.

Humankind needs to enter into an ablation procedure where we extirpate affliction as the motivator of politics, economy, health, education and beliefs. We need surgery, we need to wake up from the deep nightmare of fear we have been co-creating. Free from affliction we can discern the simplest and easiest way to produce change in our own field of experience. The person who knows what life means is not afraid of death, because he or she knows that death is birth, and no one can exterminate consciousness. It will continue to create life.

We are only one spoke of the spinning wheel of incarnations. Anarchy, chaos is part of the experience of rebirthing society. There is no birth that can occur without death, there is no imperfection in the process—it is a natural cycle. One who understands this does not fear change.

I believe we can weave a different tapestry with different colors and patterns. I believe we can unweave undesired knots in the tapestry. I believe we can live as a society that is harmonious, balanced, and inclusive. I believe that humans are capable of creating beauty and art. I believe humanity can create the technology to regenerate the resources of the earth, making for sustainable forms of living. I believe that people are capable of giving birth to wise and intelligent choices, and that consciousness can help us evolve. I believe that we can have an economy based in wellbeing and abundance. I believe that resilience, endurance and persistence can bring about miracles. I believe that our capacity for unconditional love is the motivation and the purpose of life. But will this potential reality be knitted into the tapestry of our species history? This I cannot say.

But every day as I open my eyes I choose to realize that this miracle has already taken place.

NITAMO FEDERICO MONTECUCCO

Laszlo Institute of New Paradigm Research

The change of an era, the transition we are now experiencing from a divided, polluted and war-torn world based on rage and dominance, and fear and submission to a globalized, sustainable and peaceful planet based on kindness and care and the recognition of human dignity—this transition requires new modes of thought, a new consciousness.

Our psychosomatic unity and wellbeing is possible because every cell in our body has the same DNA, the same information. Knowledge and awareness is the recognition that we are part of humanity, of one and the same living system. The new paradigm is becoming a shared scientific and cultural, a truly planetary DNA. It is the basic knowledge and recognition of our multicultural humanity on earth. Consciousness is the heart of every living being, self-awareness is the new frontier of human evolution, and consciousness together with self-awareness are at the core of the new paradigm.

In the last decades an exponentially growing number of people have been experiencing states of deeper consciousness and self-awareness, achieved through meditation and mindfulness. More and more people are undergoing emotional and psychological transformation, becoming oriented to a more ecological, equitable, rightful and peaceful society. For the first time in history, the internet, media and cellular communications are creating a planetary web, a global neural network: a planetary consciousness. People are becoming aware that the paradigm that had hitherto dominated society is obsolete and ecologically, culturally and socially unsustainable. They are ready to shift to a more sustainable, nonviolent, natural and humane paradigm. Human intelligence is undergoing a period of transformation; a trial of new approaches and new modes of thought and action.

An exponentially increasing number of researches on consciousness has been published In the last fifteen years in scientific journals in the neurosciences, medicine, psychology and education. Over 2,500 studies (listed in PubMed) demonstrate the clinical efficacy of mindfulness and self-awareness in the reduction of: stress, cortisol (the stress hormone), testosterone (aggressiveness), depression, muscular and psychic tension, insomnia, hypertension, chronic pain and inflammation, hypertension, cardiovascular disease, cancer, lung diseases, headache, sleep disorders, anxiety disorders, panic attacks, digestive disorders (colitis, gastritis), as well as impaired memory and concentration. Research shows that practices of self-awareness improve the climate in every group or class, creating, empathy, trust and collaboration, reducing aggressiveness and bullying, and improves concentration, self-esteem and performance in school. Thousands of neuroscience projects of research have shown that already being in a state of self-awareness, such as mindfulness and meditation, transforms neuronal, hormonal and emotional circuits, and changes the way we behave, relate and think. Self-awareness generates an inner, behavioral, emotional and cognitive revolution that enables each person to change himself or herself, and his or her relations to the world.

The new paradigm does not offer ready-made answers and solutions, but highlights a different way of dealing with and resolving problems through a change in self-awareness, creating a new consciousness for a new era. Based on self-awareness and global understanding, the new paradigm can be taught, and it can be acquired by everyone. We can all foster the evolution of our consciousness and cooperate in the creation of a better world.

STEPHAN A. SCHWARTZ

Saybrook University

What will the future be like? Media plays back to us our dystopian Zeitgeist about the future seen from the second decade of the 21st century. And the scenario dispassionately based on science does indeed look very challenging. Considering sea rise alone, we are going to experience massive change disrupting the lives of hundreds of millions of people. And that is only one aspect of the changes coming. The choice we face now is: how are we going to react to what will be happening?

One thing we cannot do for certain is accurately predict our technological future. Consider: In 1935, in the middle of the Great Depression, Franklin Roosevelt put together a blue ribbon panel of scientists and other academicians. He gave them one task: Look 27 years into the future, to 1952, and give the government, give me, the most insightful, the most fact-based assessment you can render of what that America will be like. At that time, it seemed reasonable that the president could get a reliable answer. Science seemed on the verge of solving most problems, and to extrapolate from the known present to a future less than three decades down the line was well within an individual lifetime. It seemed doable.

The panel worked very seriously on their forecast; on reading it, the erudition and thoughtfulness of the group is apparent. However, there are a few things missing from their predictions. They had no thought of jet aircraft, nuclear energy, the atomic bomb, antibiotics, television, or Alan Turing s computer. Even in their most free-form speculation, they could not foresee the technologies that lay just twenty plus years in the future. The major lesson of their report, seen in retrospect: predicting technological and social specifics is not a very helpful way to prepare for the future. What then is?

As it happens, new research breakthroughs which collectively argue that all life is interconnected and interdependent, and that consciousness is not entirely physiologically based, that an aspect of it exists that is nonlocal, and that change in consciousness constitutes the fundamental leverage point— these are beginning to give us some useful guidance: we have to change our culture, give up focusing on the how. Instead, we must change our culture to make wellbeing the first priority, from the individual to the family, community, nation and the planetary community. Wellness oriented social policies are cheaper, more effective, more productive, more equitable, nicer to live under, and more enduring. And that's just a partial list. The evidence by a wide spectrum of social outcome measures is overwhelming. This transition is already proving that the life-affirming choice can be profitable. Make no mistake, enormous fortunes are going to be made creating a world that works with the earth s great meta-systems in consciousness-based life-affirming ways, just as billionaires were birthed like puppies as the digital world came into being.

We are going to have to make this change. We cannot dominate the earth s meta-systems; climate change is teaching us that. We must learn to work with them, learn how to work with life in an affirming manner including recognizing the reality and the role of consciousness. And ultimately we will; it is the only way a non-dystopian future can occur. So the real question is, how much pain are we willing to inflict on ourselves before we change our culture? Culture created climate change. Culture can fix it. And the key to changing culture is the Quotidian Choice, the thousands of small daily choices we each make, of which we are mostly unconscious. When enough of us make the same choice, culture changes. Look at the transition from Gay to LGBT (lesbian, gay, bisexual, and transgender). It is not just a change in the words one uses, it is a change in attitude. Look at what has happened in the decline of smoking. Be aware of how solar power is growing as family after family seeks a personal alternative to their dependence on carbon energy. And we have some evidence as to how many people it takes to put wellbeing first, effectively.

A study by the Social Cognitive Networks Academic Research Center (SCNARC) at Rensselaer Polytechnic Institute provides data-based guidance: "To change the beliefs of an entire community, only 10% of the population needs to become convinced of a new or different opinion. At that tipping point, the idea can spread through social networks and alter behavior on a large scale."

As a society, we need to recognize that all life is interconnected and interdependent, and consciousness is underlying all. As Max Planck, the father of Quantum Mechanics told us in 1931, "I regard consciousness as fundamental. I regard matter as derivative from consciousness. We cannot get behind consciousness. Everything that we talk about, everything that we regard as existing postulates consciousness." We must make wellbeing the first priority. And the way to do that is not complicated, nor does it require official position, power, or wealth. Become aware when you are making a choice of the options available to you, and choose the one that is the most compassionate and life-affirming, as you understand it. When 10 percent of us choose in this way, we will take the most effective, cheapest, most efficient, and most life-affirming path into the future.

ZHI GANG SHA

Spiritual teacher

Change can be painful and change is inevitable. It has been said that change is the one constant in life. As a Tao servant and teacher, I would like to add that change is The Way. Change is a universal law. As we experience and observe the current turbulent world changes, it is helpful to remember what the legendary Tao sage, Lao Tzu taught about the concept of creation and reverse creation. The natural cycle of existence is creation and reverse creation. In the transition between these two cycles, many people experience great anxiety, fear and frustration. Instead of succumbing to those emotions, we can shift our consciousness to how we can facilitate the change for the good, and we can empower others to do the same.

Mother Earth is in great distress. Much of humanity is in deep suffering mentally, emotionally, physically, financially, in their relationships and more, and the future may look very bleak at this moment. Before a paradigm shift and positive change comes enormous, if not complete, breakdown of all existing structures. Being on Mother Earth at this time, it is our responsibility and privilege to be the light agents to help birth a new world.

We cannot make significant progress by working on the physical level alone. The Tao teaches us that true, lasting change must come from the soul.

Soul moves, heart moves.
Heart moves, consciousness moves.
Consciousness moves, energy moves.
Energy moves, matter moves.

The soul has power to transform every aspect of life. To understand and use this knowledge is how we can arise out of darkness and despair. Much ancient wisdom and practice focus on three sacred words: jing, qi, and shen. "Jing" means matter. "Qi" (pronounced *chee*) means energy. "Shen" (pronounced *shun*) encompasses soul, heart, and mind. Everyone and everything is made of jing qi shen.

For centuries, scientists have sought a "theory of everything"—one set of universal principles and laws that can explain everything in the physical universe. It is the time to unite the physical world and the spiritual world as one. Science and spirituality can meld as one if they can reach a common understanding of information and soul. With this understanding, we will be able to connect and transform all aspects of life into a harmonious whole.

How do we accomplish this? By living and spreading the ten Da, the ten greatest qualities that are the nature of the Divine and Tao. The ten Da are the spiritual and practical keys to transforming every aspect of life. When one practices and lives according to the ten Da qualities, one is transformed, and everyone and everything they connect with are also changed for the better.

In this brief sketch I will only describe the first and the most important Da quality, Da Ai, or *Greatest Love*. "Da" means greatest. "Ai" means love. "Da Ai" means *greatest love*. Love melts all blockages and transforms all life. Da Ai is the greatest healer to heal all kinds of sickness, including sickness in the physical body, emotional body, mental body, and spiritual body. Da Ai can transform your finances and business; it can transform all kinds of relationships. Da Ai can open one's heart and soul. Da Ai can increase wisdom and intelligence. Da Ai can open one's spiritual channels. Da Ai can transform all life.

Ancient teaching is that success and disaster happen at the same time. Let us consider the current situation a time of great opportunity. This is the time to step up to change the world and all humanity to be peaceful, loving and harmonious. It *can* be done. The choice is ours. The time is now.

GARY ZUKAV

The Seat of the Soul Institute

Rage is a form of fear. Moving beyond rage requires moving beyond the control of fear. Anger, jealousy, vengefulness, depression, obsessive thoughts, compulsive activities, and addictive behaviors are also forms of fear. It may seem an unwarranted leap to apply emotional and behavioral terms to "science," but science without awareness of intentions now has no future.

There are two bedrock intentions: love and fear. All that is not love is fear. All that is not fear is love. Intentions determine consequences. Human perception is expanding beyond the domain of the five senses—the empirical domain. Millions of humans are beginning to sense the physical universe as less than the totality of their experience. They are beginning to experience themselves as more than minds and bodies, their experiences as more than random, and the Universe as alive, wise, and compassionate.

All of this bears directly on empirical science. It makes it analogous to classical physics. Classical physics was once considered the entire context of physics and is now, following the discoveries of quantum physics, relegated to the status of a "special limiting case." This analogy has a major flaw: classical physics (the special limiting case) can be practiced unimpaired by the development of subatomic physics. However, science without awareness of intention is now counterproductive to human evolution and probably to human survival.

The empirical understanding of intention is straightforward. The intention to build an object creates an object. As human perception expands beyond the empirical, the critical question becomes, "What is the intention behind building the object?" The five sensory (empirical) domain of time, space, matter, and duality, physical causes produce physical effects. In the new expanded domain of human perception—multi-sensory perception—the nonphysical motivation behind the deed or action (the intention of love or the intention of fear) creates consequences. These consequences shape the experiences of the one who intends.

The intention of love (for example, to contribute to the well-being of another) produces constructive and healthy consequences. The intention of fear (for example, to manipulate or control another for self-benefit) creates destructive and unhealthy consequences. Therefore, the same action can have different intentions. Only the intender knows the intention. The action may be writing a check to a charity. The intention behind the action may be to create a tax deduction, to be seen as a philanthropist, to think better of oneself, or to feed hungry children. The latter intention comes from love. The former intentions come from fear. All produce different consequences.

From the special limiting case of five-sensory perception, the consequence is the same regardless of intention: the charity receives money, and children are fed. Multi-sensory perception illuminates a different vista. If the intention is to give in order to benefit oneself (an intention of fear), the one who gives will experience others self-benefitting from their "gifts" to him. In other words, he will be manipulated by others who also are motivated by self-gain.

Power in the special limiting case of five sensory perception is the ability to manipulate and control. This is external power. Power from the multi-sensory perspective is alignment of the personality with the soul, or in behavioral terms, harmony, cooperation, sharing, and reverence for life. This is authentic power. Pursuit of external power now produces only violence and destruction. Science without this perspective now threatens our evolution. In other words, it is no longer productive to practice the science of the special limiting case (empirical science) while pretending that we are not becoming multi-sensory and sensing and seeing all that we are. It is toxic and dangerous.

Creating a science without fear is necessary for our future. However, science without fear cannot be created by a fearful scientist. Is she practicing science to publish, for admiration, to gain recognition, to obtain tenure, or is she following her heart? She creates consensus results in all cases, and at the same time creates more significant spiritual results that are determined by her intentions—constructive when her intention comes from love and destructive when it comes from fear. This occurs whether she is experimenting in the laboratory or shopping for groceries. Her intentions contribute love or fear in each of the many collectives in which she participates—family, community, culture, nation, religion, gender, and the collective consciousness of humankind.

Scientists are seekers of truth. Our new evolutionary modality, multisensory perception, and understanding of power all require that we seek it in our lives, and our lives are our laboratories. The new science will be much more dramatically different from the old than quantum physics is from classical physics. It will be the science of the heart, not the science of the intellect. The heart will be the Director of Research. The intellect will be a research assistant. And all the results will be verifiable in the laboratory of life and communicable to other scientists.

COMMENTS FROM THE LASZLO INSTITUTE OF NEW PARADIGM RESEARCH*

* www.laszloinstitute.com

ANTON J. G. BILTON

Patron

Much like a homing-pigeon, we possess an instinct to reconnect to our source—to the Cosmic Mind from where the spark of divinity that lies within each of us had originally emerged.

This instinct—like a radar pulse—is now stronger than ever as our connection to that Cosmic Mind and thus, by implication to each other and to nature, is sending alarm bells to "wake up" and recognize the impending ecological catastrophe we have provoked.

By means of meditation, prayer, natural medicines and even psychedelics, people across the globe are experiencing a personal awakening and are remembering their connection to each other, to nature, and to the source of their existence.

Quantum physics has enabled us to see the effect of the observer on the observed; to recognize that mind affects matter; and to accept that matter may be no more than the pimpernel on the skin of existence. The manifestation of matter by the Cosmic Mind may be only to provide a platform for our sensory experience, to allow this Mind to experience through us its potential and to provide the checks and balances of its own morality by sharing with us the experience of suffering and of compassion.

As this volume exemplifies, pioneering scientific and spiritual visionaries across the globe are responding to the alarm bells and prompting us to re-awaken to the interconnectivity that pervades all things. With their help, we are awakening to a wisdom we had always possessed. We must grasp this wisdom, propagate its insights, and consciously and decisively act to avert the crisis that looms ahead.

There simply is no separation nor separateness in the world, and by focusing on this understanding with compassion, and with the active endeavor it inspires, we can save our planet.

This is a new Renaissance and it is one we must welcome in these critical times.

LAWRENCE BLOOM

Patron

Letter from Vilcabamba (Equador). I have just spent three days with two Mamos from the Kogi and We Wa peoples of the Four Nations. These are the people who successfully evaded the Conquistadors by living in the high Sierra Nevada mountains at Santa Marta. They are a dreaming culture totally uncontaminated by any Western influence. Their culture is many thousands of years old. The Four Nations base their lifestyles on their belief in "Aluna" or "The Great Mother," their creator figure, whom they believe is the force behind nature. They understand the earth to be a living being, and see humanity as its "children." They say that our actions of exploitation, devastation, and plundering for resources is weakening "The Great Mother" and leading to our destruction.

From birth they attune their priests, called *Mamos* (which means sun in Kogi), for guidance, healing, and leadership. The Mamas are not to be confused with shamans or curers but to be regarded as tribal priests who hold highly respected roles in their society. Mamas undergo strict training to assume this role. Selected male children are taken from birth and put in a dark cave from the age of three. They may stay there for up to twenty-five years of their lives to experience this training. In the cave, elder Mamos and the child's mother care for, feed, train, and teach the child to attune to "Aluna" before the boy enters the outside world. Can you imagine the level of sensitivity these Mamos experience? They feel the pain of Gaia in locations thousands of miles away.

Their calculation of the Mayan long count was that it ended in May 2013. That means that we have thirteen years to shift our consciousness, and indeed the lens through which we see the world. They see three converging crises, financial, social and environmental. They recognize that they look separate but suggest that they stem from a common cause, which is a crisis in values. Even that crisis stems from a still deeper one. These crises are the lens through which we view the world. Through this lens we have lost our connection with the earth that gives us life, the cosmos that gave us birth, and also from each other. Yet without each other our lives have no meaning.. and we have also disconnected from our own true nature. According to Mamos, and some other profound mystics that it is my privilege to know, we have therefore nine years left to shift our consciousness from separation to connection. This is not long. Most environmental experts give us twenty years to get this right. However, interestingly enough some of my friends in finance are not optimistic and tend to agree with the shorter horizon. So "what to do?" as my Indian friends would say.

I am working with many leading thinkers and investors to create an Office for the Future at the UN. This office will focus not on what is breaking down but on what is breaking through. It will focus and look for breakthroughs in the sectors provided by the sustainable development goals. Over one million people contributed to their creation. In September 2015 at the UN in New York, global leaders committed to achieving 17 Sustainable Development Goals by 2030. In December 2015 at COP-21 in Paris, global leaders concluded a climate agreement to significantly reduce greenhouse gas emissions, and this agreement officially went into effect worldwide at COP-22 in Marrakesh. For the first time in the history, every nation without exception voted for it.

We are midwives to a new age. We need to see what is wanting to be "born" in the sectors of poverty alleviation, health, education, energy, oceans, safe and resilient cities and others. We need to protect and nurture this emergence politically, socially, economically and financially. This office can be replicated eventually in every community on earth. Some breakthroughs might only have local significance, others will be both replicable and expandable globally. For the first time, we as a species, could become conscious of our own emergence. As my colleague, Barbara Marx Hubbard observed, we will be moving from unconscious co-creation to conscious co-creation. We have the technology and there is the emerging crisis. The belief that we only have nine years is an eye opener, but even if we have a little longer (which I don't believe), it would be best to start now.

We are moving from an Age of Change to a Change of Age, and it's going to be a bumpy ride!

NICOLYA CHRISTI

Director, WorldShift Program

Everything we have understood about ourselves and the world is undergoing a radical transformation. The winds of evolutionary change are upon us. Humanity is slowly beginning to emerge from a long and sustained period of ignorance and darkness. As conscious evolutionaries, ecologists and humanitarians, we are beginning to witness the influence of awakened consciousness as it permeates the bedrock of the old paradigm. As this infiltrates the very foundations of the "matrix," the greatest potential for whole system change, from the inside out, is now becoming a tangible possibility. As the destructive trajectory of the old world increases on a daily basis, so too does the exponential awakening of consciousness within the heart of humanity.

The forces of light and dark are meeting now, as evidenced by the unparalleled events to have transpired at Standing Rock. First Nations prophecy states the following: *"Under the symbol of the Rainbow, all of the races and all of the religions of the world will band together. After a great struggle, using only the force of peace, rainbow warriors will finally bring an end to the destruction and desecration of Mother Earth."* These ancient words are a reference to our present times.

The human race has arrived at a critical juncture, an existential turning point. Its core wounds of polarity, separation, disconnection and duality have been undeniably exposed, especially, and most spectacularly, during the recent US presidential electoral campaign. The campaign revealed the full extent of the cracks within the foundation stones of unconscious global leadership. The wave-field effect of the 2016 US electoral campaign and the newly elected US president have marked an evolutionary turning point for humanity and serve as a divinely timed catalyst for a necessary shift to occur within the collective consciousness and for global transformation. The current system of leadership throughout the world is in crisis and we are now called to step up and step out to begin the co-creation of a conscious new paradigm. It is time to trust that we are ready to fulfill our roles as the midwives of a conscious new epoch.

The lens through which we view social, political, economic, and environmental issues determines the degree to which we become locked in uncertainty and fear or centered in gnosis and trust. We teeter on the threshold of both the old and the new, and so we need to remain vigilant and mindful not to default into fear, duality, rage, uncertainty, separation, powerlessness or an *"us versus them"* mentality. It is time to walk our talk as empowered visionaries and transformers of consciousness. We have waited our entire lives to arrive at this specific moment on the timeline of humanity. It is upon us now to become fully visible, present and active as transformers of personal and planetary consciousness, anchored in love, peace, unity, gnosis and trust.

We are at the End Times. It really is the dark before the light of dawn, the storm before the calm. The world as we know it is dying and a new world is being born. Just as a fever peaks before it breaks so it is that the fever of dysfunctional global governance has finally reached break point. We are not powerless yet empowered beyond measure, when we join together in service of world peace and harmony. If we polarize in fear, we remain part of the problem but by rooting ourselves in trust we become part of the solution. Now, more than ever before, we need to stand together in and as love, expressing the deepest wisdom, holding the highest vision and applying the purest altruism to our every thought, word, action and deed. The road ahead of us may not be an easy one yet we are more prepared now than at any other time for what is to come, who we must be, and what we must do.

Humanity has been moving through *the eye of the needle,* a rare cosmic phenomenon referred to as "The Galactic Alignment Zone," which began in 1975 and concludes in 2021. A thirty-six-year window of time, known as "The Galactic Alignment," formed its epicenter. Beginning on the Winter Solstice of 1980 and drawing to a close on December 21, 2016, it catalyzed an exponential spiritual awakening and acceleration in conscious evolution. However, it is only when the Galactic Alignment Zone completes on the Winter Solstice of 2021 that humanity will witness the first indications of a new conscious epoch becoming a tangible reality.

ERVIN LASZLO

It is unconditional love, unity consciousness, and futuristic technology that will carry humanity into a new conscious paradigm and a harmonious, peaceful and sustainable world. The greatest gift we can offer to the world at this time is to *remember who we truly are* and *what we truly know*. No force is mightier than an awakened, conscious, unified, empowered and enlightened humanity that is rooted in uncompromising, unwavering and unequivocal love, wisdom and truth. Let us remember that we are 7.4 billion people. We are the macrocosm, not the insignificant microcosm. When we join together in and as enlightened consciousness, we can move mountains to manifest world peace. The destiny of humanity is in our hands and never will so much have been achieved by so few for so many.

Collectively, we seem to have understood that the imperative is to position ourselves in unity consciousness and refuse to be part of any expression that supports even an iota of separation. *What remains essential in all of this is the need for us to work together, to align in Oneness and Greater Purpose, and commit fully, not only to supporting, but to becoming part of the co-creation of a world that manifests the insights of the new evolutionary paradigm.*

NORA CSISZAR

Director, Communications and Public Relations

The term "Millennial" is used in the mainstream media to place anyone born between the early 1980s and the late 2000s into the same category, often trying to compare and contrast the differences between them and the previous generations (known as the Baby Boomers and Gen X), The Millennials and are often criticized as being lazy, flaky, self-obsessed ne'er-do-wells. Older generations condemn the Millennials, even though they are a large and diverse group of talented and hard-working individuals not all that different from those who came before them.

As a Millennial myself, I have heard all my life that the world and humanity are constantly in danger because of ongoing environmental, social, economic and political crises. It is clear to me that the old paradigm is no longer functioning well— and in fact, it is no longer needed—and a new and higher consciousness must arise to deal with the challenges we face, ranging from climate change and large-scale industrial pollution to unstable and un-trustworthy companies and institutions causing economic fallouts such as unemployment and bankruptcy—not to mention the common threat of terrorism and a human population that grows while many other species are becoming extinct. Millennials are both idealistic and pragmatic, they know that they will be around long enough to have to deal with such issues.

Currently there is a great deal of frustration, anger and fear. The media are only making things worse by spreading anxiety, stress and depression among people. As a trained psychologist, I know that there are many reasons why people feel, think and behave in this way, but we must not forget that there is also a real longing for something better, and a sincere hope that change will come soon. It can be difficult to keep a positive mindset and not let the bad things in the world affect our inner state. We must stay focused, happy, and even grateful. Many times I have been called naïve, idealistic, and opinionated. Well, as a member of a generation that has no problem speaking its mind and questioning the "truths" and expectations of the previous generation, I offer here my message.

We of the Millennial generation are full of passion, excitement, and uniqueness. We are carving our own paths and our own way of doing things. We are fearless, bold, and know that we have amazing opportunities to make a positive difference in the world by having our voice heard and our ideas brought to realization. We also have an incredible access to information. We can become really passionate about something, learn a great deal about it, and then go after it. We don't just want to hear others talk about how things were always done. We are interested in how things actually work…and how they could work better. Millennials are ready to go out and find their passion; they really want to change the world. They have hope for a better future. And hope is always a good thing.

If I were to pick out negative things about us Millennials, I would say that sometimes we are too concerned by the current state of the world. We set high standards for ourselves, and because of that we get insecure and worry that our own hard work will not be enough to make a difference.

Most of us know that the world is fragile in many ways. War and destruction are the main polarizers, as well as the profit-driven greed of corporations and of oligarchs. We truly care about the environment, and know that climate change is a man-made problem and we need to solve it by holding peaceful protests, choosing environmentally friendly products, recycling our resources, using public transportation whenever possible, and demanding sustainable practices in local and global business.

Hopefully, we the Millennials who are now living through the turbulence of the latest elections will soon be candidates for political office in the future and will change how things are done, working together for shared goals. We will be able to do so, because we accept people of different races, sexual identities and religions, embracing the differences among them. We are the least judgmental generation. We accept new norms and refuse to live in a segregated, sexist, racist, homophobic and xenophobic world.

We Millennials are a lot more informed than any previous generation has been, thanks to the new media. The internet has not only connected the world around us as never before, but has also provided us with seemingly unlimited information and the capacity to share it. With the amount of information and data that are now available, we can bring about a real change for the better in the world.

A word in conclusion. We Millennials have been taught by the greatest minds in history. We saw the mistakes made by those who came before us, and we do not intend to repeat them. Fortunately, we have great role models as well, people who are not only amazing, smart, and totally cool themselves, but inspire us to become better persons and help each other. We experience the urge to find and reinvent ourselves and to explore what the world has to offer, but we also want to find out what we can offer to the world. We embrace all of humankind, because we know that everybody's future depends on it, including our own. We are focusing on how we can fix the world by saving it from the mess it is already in. Don't worry, we will fix it, but we need the cooperation of all living generations in order to pull together and do it!

https://www2.deloitte.com/us/en/pages/about-deloitte/articles/millennial-majority-transform-ing-culture.html

http://iop.harvard.edu/iop-now/millennials-global-warming

http://www.recyclingtoday.com/article/cox-consereves-millennials-sustainability-survey/

http://time.com/247/millennials-the-me-me-me-generation/

KINGSLEY L. DENNIS

Director, Publishing Program

(See "Messages by the Authors of *What Is Reality*," above)

SHAMIK DESAI

Director, Special Programs

(See "Messages by the Authors of *What Is Reality*," above)

CHRISTINE CLARE COLLINS

Managing Editor, *World Futures: The Journal of New*

Paradigm Research

Imagine there's no heaven
It's easy if you try
No hell below us
Above us only sky
Imagine all the people living for today ... *

This is a call for all those who imagine, those who dare to imagine topographies where the terrain escapes dark dimensions that form from manifestations of perceived difference and hate ...

To imagine is the mantra of the artist, the dreamer ... the poet, the crafter of myths, narratives, and film—and it is their power—to pave the way forward into a new reality ... in the face of linear, hierarchal grasslands and deserts planted and strewn so firmly here centuries ago by a Cartesian wave that washed over the world to form a male fellowship that controlled a "Clockwork Universe," one that sought to separate mind from body, and soul from cosmic consciousness.

Imagine there's no countries
It isn't hard to do
Nothing to kill or die for
And no religion too
Imagine all the people living life in peace ...

---

*   Lennon, J. *Imagine*. New York: Downtown Music Publishing, 1971.

The universe, the true womb of humankind knows no nationality ... knows no "walls" or ideological boundaries that cause war ... We all so dread those places where territories are cruelly formed through crystallizations of greed, racism, misogyny ...

We lie in wait for the artist to draw new maps of reality through a mythopoeic impulse to disassemble and rearrange the crumbling stone walls built by the men of old. From this chaos, order will be formed ... and we will be sustained as one people, living in one world—forging toward a one-way highway that's baptized as a reorientation toward love ... and dubbed simple PEACE ... Yes ... peace.

> *You may say I'm a dreamer*
> *But I'm not the only one*
> *I hope someday you'll join us*
> *And the world will be as one*

Many have been asking, "Who are the dreamers and where have they gone?" Are they above us ... crying the tears that we feel and hear and taste in our repulsion as we attempt to emerge from these days of such shaming, bullying and separation: women/men, black/white, gay/straight, Christian and Jew and Muslim and ... ...

We call to the artists ... those among us who dare to imagine ... to lead us forth to a new reality ... towards the place of light and integral consciousness.

To do so ... would truly make the dreamer imagine a new map of reality that is ... No, not just for you and me ... but for us ... and not just for today ... but for tomorrow and ... for always.

ERVIN LASZLO

Director

(See "Messages by the Authors of *What Is Reality*," above)

NITAMO FEDERICO MONTECUCCO

Dean, the Gaia University Program

(See "Messages by the Authors of *What Is Reality*," above)

ALFONSO MONTUORI

Associate Editor, *World Futures: the Journal of*

New Paradigm Research

Times of transition such as ours bring on tremendous insecurity. They can lead to fear and rage as the world we once knew disappears. It is tempting for some to want to go back to the "good old days" of security, when we knew "what was what," when there was a semblance of order and predictability in the world, when people knew their place. We see in recent political developments the incredible tension between a desire for change and wanting to cling on to tradition, and the way in which hopes and fears can be manipulated and channeled into rage.

Our age has been called post-normal, meaning that everything is changing and nothing is "normal" anymore. I believe it is also the case that in the West we are currently in a "post-progress" society, one that is incapable of envisioning better worlds. The word progress seems to have disappeared from our vocabulary, and the future is viewed in terms of sustainability and the ability to avoid catastrophic changes, whether ecological, social, or political. Young people are told they will likely earn less than their parents, and their prospects are bleak: the Millennial Generation, bigger than even the enormously influential Baby Boomer generation, has also been called Generation Screwed. Many find it hard to even conceive of the notion of a "better" future.

At this time of transition, we are facing a crisis of the future. Few scenarios inspire, let alone point to, the kind of transformation we need. Staying the same is "unsustainable," attempting "sustainability" is necessary if uninspiring, returning to a previous age (romanticizing a past that never existed) is impossible—it is but a popular form of deception and manipulation—but for many there is little that motivates us to move forward. Motivationally, we want to avoid disaster. We are not drawn to any future that would be better.

This is a complex crisis, which requires a radical (in its etymological sense of going to the roots) approach. How we think about and work for the future, and what we think constitutes progress are key issues. But what comes next? We cannot predict it. We can envision possible scenarios, so we can be prepared, but that is not enough. The key in my view is a re-cognition of our creativity, which is how we got here, and how we will both envision alternatives and make them into realities.

Our understanding and practice of creativity also need radical revision. In the old Machine Paradigm creativity was an unusual phenomenon, limited to gifted, exceptional, isolated individuals. In the new paradigm, creativity and interconnectedness are key features of the Universe. If creativity is the very nature of the Universe, we are creatures and creators, indeed co-creators in an interconnected Universe. The question then becomes not "can I/we create," or "but what am I/are we creating?" And how can we "re-cognize" our own creativity, our own interconnectedness, and take responsibility for it? How can we mobilize grass-roots creativity to envision better futures that are better for everybody, and make them real? How can we re-create our world together in a way that reflects unity in diversity?

There is a quotation, attributed to Einstein, that a problem cannot be solved from the same level of consciousness that created it. In that spirit, we cannot envision and create a new world with the same kind of atomistic creativity that created the Industrial-Machine world. We need to challenge our old views of the future, of progress and creativity and of what it means to be human, and re-imagine them to re-create our world. We need to break down the split between theory and practice and recognize the extent to which all our practices are infused with misguided Machine-paradigm concepts of the world. At the same time as we continue to act we need to reflect, we need to unlearn as we learn and perform as we practice. We need to reach out to others to join us on our journey of co-creation with the profound awareness that we are all in the same boat, and that time is running out for saving ourselves in this sinking boat.

JOE ST. CLAIR

Executive Director

One of the greatest challenges we now collectively face as a species is to have the courage to re-examine ourselves from a heart-centered perspective rather than using the long established head-centered rationality we were taught at school. This is an exceptionally difficult thing to do because it challenges one of the most fundamental pillars of our society. It challenges our identity and our status as *"homo economicus"*—the term coined by classical economists to homogeneously define "us" as a species—and our place in the world. The whole science of economics is based on a theoretical model of human behavior that defines all of us as "rational economic agents" who make decisions based only on internal "value calculations" when choosing between alternatives. This approach has been known as "utilitarianism" by economists since the early nineteenth century. In other words, according to the classical economist we always choose pleasure over pain and we always buy the commodities that selfishly maximizes our own personal welfare even if others suffer as a consequence. This belief lies at the core of all economic theory and drives the way everything is done. Worryingly, it also drives the way governments make decisions, companies make profits and banks lend money. And also, we are told confidently by the "experts," it drives the way cultures, society and individuals consistently behave.

This means that the way classical economists view our place in the world is very simple. We are the species *"homo economicus,"* who possess an "economic resource" called earth. This economic model has become sacrosanct—an "unquestionable truth" that underpins everything we do and influences every decision we make. To the economist we are simply walking statistics labelled "consumers." Our destiny is to derive pleasure from consuming (and preferably consuming more than our competitors, according to economic theorists) and we have an abundant and seemingly endless supply of resources to exploit for our personal benefit. We have access to a rich storehouse of so-called "natural resources" that is just waiting for us to plunder at will. It is an infinite provider of clean water, abundant food, rich minerals, endless forests and pure air—it is called planet Earth.

The problem is that the old paradigm's classical way of viewing the way we behave as a species poses one of the biggest and most significant threats to our future, and the future of our planet.

In other words, the modern global economic model that defines how we supposedly "think" does not allow for alternatives that would challenge its 200-year supremacy. For that reason it has not yet recognized the single biggest flaw in its logic. This flaw is that *"homo economicus"* i.e. you and I, do not always make rational, logical decisions based on "maximizing" our welfare and status and rewarding our pockets and our ego. To the horror of economic experts, some of us actually make decisions based on selflessness, empathy, love, compassion, kindness, generosity, passion and caring. This sort of behavior is statistically ignored by economists who label it an "irrational aberration" in the economic model. In short, modern economics can survive as a framework for organized society only as long as it continues to deny, suppress and denigrate the idea that *"homo economicus"* could have any form of compassion, connectedness, spirituality, and connection with a Divine spirit.

But subtly, and almost imperceptibly, things are changing. The "establishment", which has held on to power by endorsing and upholding the classical economic model as the Holy Grail of "progress," is getting increasingly worried. The long-chanted mantras of "economic growth", "perfect competition", "sustained consumerism" and "self-adjusting markets" now ring hollow as outmoded and no longer accepted truths. In short, the system is broken and the old guard and the old paradigm are choking on their own words.

The growth of the "environmental movement" over the last 25 years, for example, now poses one of the most significant threats to the established economic worldview. If this this wasn't bad enough, some other pillars of the old paradigm model are also starting to crumble. Unpredicted economic slowdown and stagnation is rocking the world financial markets, the belief that "science can solve everything' is waning, inequality and poverty is rife, human rights are still being ignored, crime and unemployment is rising, depression and suicide levels are rocketing, endangered species are dying out due to loss of habitat and pollution, and deforestation is destabilizing climatic patterns and leading to catastrophic climate change. War, terrorism and civil unrest is rife across the world. Little wonder that poor *"homo economicus'* feels increasingly isolated, bewildered and directionless.

Even though repeated studies by independent researchers continue to reveal that most economic forecasts are consistently wrong, we still stubbornly cling to "old-world" views because we do not seem to have any workable and realistic alternatives. Old paradigm economics, unfortunately, still offer governments, particularly Neoliberals, a slowly deteriorating "comfort blanket" to which to cling.

As Paul Mason succinctly puts it in his book *Postcapitalism*, *"The long term prospects for capitalism are bleak. According to the OECD, growth in the developed world will be 'weak' for the next 50 years. Inequality will rise by 40%. For the developed world the best of capitalism is behind us. For the rest it will be over in our lifetime."*

This is the new, if unpalatable, reality. The Neoliberalist dream, and the doctrine of uncontrolled markets with individual consumers pursuing their own self-interests is in rapid decline and will soon self-implode. So what does this actually mean for us and our times? It means we are about to enter "uncharted waters", and there is no government on earth that can provide us with answers or direction because, as the recent US elections and the Brexit debacle have demonstrated, we live in unprecedented and unstable times.

Where does this leave us? Is it a case of "Abandon hope all ye who enter here"? My belief is that there is unquestionably cause for hope—thanks to our inherent and indomitable human spirit. All over the world there are isolated pockets of like-minded individuals slowly but determinedly coming together and saying "enough is enough".

At the cutting edge of quantum physics there are convergences with the latest research into the molecular and energetic vibrational fields of our biological bodies. And what is being discovered is not just astonishing; it is game changing. At the fundamental quantum level we are exactly what the Eastern Mystics have tried to teach the West for centuries. We are vibrational waves of energy that are intimately connected to everything around us, including rocks, plants, trees, water, and our fellow human beings. Even the universe. We really are the "same stuff" as the stars. We, and everything and everyone around us are connected at the most fundamental level of our existence.

This revelation in itself is one of the most significant discoveries ever made in human history. But it is not the end of the story. Increasingly, as more and more disillusioned people search deep within themselves for meaning and purpose in their life, a steadily building undercurrent is filtering into the collective psyche. It is an inner awareness of a connection to something bigger than us. It is an inner certainty and recognition that we are more than the sum of our parts. It is an awakening realization that we are immortal beings temporarily living in an outer bodily shell. We are connected to each other and to the universe, and to a deeper source of intelligent design that some call "divinity" or "the source." The words are not important. The experience and the truth are.

These two indisputable truths—that we are all "divine beings" and that we are connected to "all that is" at a fundamental level—is very soon going to change everything. I truly believe that the days of "*homo economicus*" are virtually over and our species will shortly transition into what I would like to call "*homo Spiritus.*" This evolutionary shift has already started. I predict that it will usher in a new era where "connectedness" will substitute for "individualism" and "love" will replace "indifference".

We may still be in uncharted waters, but our collective spiritual compasses have started to kick in. I think the transition has already started.

GYORGYI SZABO

Director of Research

Our hyper-complex world is fraught with countless social and environmental challenges that fill us with anxiety and fear—for the present as well as for the future. Most people wish to have a peaceful and compassionate world, but they are unsure what to do to create it and where to begin. Is entrusting external sources such as governments and social leaders the only thing we can do? Hardly so. Entrusting and enacting one's own abilities brings far greater change than passively waiting for others to do it. We need to review who we are and of what we are capable. In order to do this, we have to start by reviewing whether the worldview that guides our life and our conduct is correct. New developments in science and the insights of Eastern philosophies offer guidance for this endeavor.

There is today a greater awareness than ever before of the countless subtleties that link diverse phenomena in the world, such as global warming, migration, world hunger, religious intolerance and social disturbance. Interconnectedness and interdependence are increasingly acknowledged, yet for individual and social change their true meaning is not fully understood and taken into consideration. Interdependence and interconnectedness on the social level mean the support of all others for our own and for everyone's survival. Every single meal we eat, each item of clothing we wear, as well as where and how we live, result from and have consequences for other people as well as for other species and nature. Because we are individually and collectively so dependent on others and the environment, we have to take care of the well-being of all people and all species so we could safeguard our own survival.

A real social transformation is only possible by personal transformation. Change begins with ourselves, our ways of life, our behaviors, aspirations and emotional responses to the issues we address. Changing the world has to proceed from the inside out.

The self-Interested Worldview versus the holistic Worldview. Self-interested behavior hallmarks the last few centuries. It stems from a worldview that alienates humans from each other, from nature and the cosmos. It considers the body as a machine in which organs and cells function as unconnected parts that can be replaced without affecting anything else in the body. It views the soul as a religious concept and sees the span of one's life as a finite and closed circuit. Selfish aims created consumerism; selfish tendencies consider us to be above nature, and one's own belief system is seen as superior to the system of others. We want to control everything and all things. We see nature as a wastebasket the same as our own body —we dump things into it indiscriminately. Large corporations produce the goods we consume; we humans are the real problem. Why are we so surprised at where we have arrived? Earth is rebelling, producing climate change; nations experience mounting crime rates as well as gender and racial inequality and increased social disobedience, ill-health is rampant, animals are hunted for trophies ... Life driven by the self-interested worldview is self-defeating and it endangers humankind the same as the planet.

For many centuries, Eastern philosophies advocated and actually lived by a holistic worldview, the view that sees all sentient and even non-sentient beings as part of a "whole" that is intrinsically and subtly interconnected, where each thing integrally affects every other. According to Eastern tenets, humans are an intrinsic part of the cosmos, and the human body is a microcosm not only governed by the same laws as the cosmos, but also animated by the same forces of growth and development. Human activities, both social and individual, model themselves on that which takes place on the macro-scale, and development in the cosmos is a model for development in the human world. The harmony of the cosmos is reflected and is maintained by harmony in the state, in the family, as well as in the body and mind of individuals. Damaging any of these harmonies disorders the whole. There is no dualism: in Eastern wisdom matter and spirit are whole and not separate, as in Western thought.

ERVIN LASZLO

Taoism, Buddhism, Hinduism are advocates of *the discovery of oneself* and of *the experience of the infinite within our self.* "There are as many infinities as there are dimensions, as many forms of liberation as there are temperaments. But all bear the same stamp. Those who suffer from bondage and confinement will experience liberation as infinite expansion. Those who suffer from darkness will experience it as light unbounded. Those who groan under the weight of death and transitoriness will feel it as eternity. Those who are restless will enjoy it as peace and infinite harmony."[3]

Mindful practices, yoga, meditation, tai chi, chi kung, and the study of wisdom traditions are among the many approaches that lead towards self-discovery. It is important to recognize that it is not material goods or financial status that make us happy and define who we are. "We do not need to buy or own anything in order to be happy. At any moment, we can access this sense of joy. The same interdependence that makes our consumerism so devastating for the environment can also make the natural environment a source of endless joy and wonder to us, without taking away anything more than a lungful of air. It just depends on how we choose to live our connectedness."[4]

Meaningful livelihood can be achieved by living consciously, based on wholesome intentions and altruistic impulses. All human action needs to benefit equally nature, society, and one's own self. To inquire into our inner world is as important as inquiring into the workings of the world around us. To truly know ourselves we have to bring our hearts and minds together while trusting our inherent wisdom. The Sufi mystic Jalaluddin Rumi said that the "entire universe is inside you." And the changes you make in you, in your universe, affect other universes. It is up to you to decide what you change, and how and when you change it. You can discover the beauty, the talent, and the magic of the universe that is YOU!

"Hear this, young men and women everywhere, and proclaim it far and wide. The Earth is yours and the fullness thereof. Be kind but be fierce. You are needed now more than ever before. Take up the mantle of change. For this is your time." A call to change and action in the social media today? It could be and should be, but it is not. It was issued by Winston Churchill in the year 1941. We would do well to remember it today, and take it to heart.

1   Howe, Neil; Strauss, William. *Generations: The History of America's Future, 1584 to 2069*. New York: William Morrow & Company, 1991..

2   Theobald, Robert. *Death and Rebirth: Explaining the Dynamics of Change*. 1999.Retrieved from https://www2.gwu.edu/~y2k/categories/y2kstudies7.html .

3   Govinda, Lama Anagarika, *Foundation of Tibetan Mysticism* (Rider&Company, U.K., 1983)

4   The Karmapa, Ogyen Trinley Dorje, *The Heart is Noble*, Changing the World from the Inside Out, Shambhala Editions, 2013.

CPSIA information can be obtained
at www.ICGtesting.com
Printed in the USA
LVOW13s1750110917
548290LV00041B/1685/P